The
Veneering
Book

The Veneering Book

DAVID SHATH SQUARE

The Taunton Press

Cover photos: TOP RIGHT, DAVID SHATH SQUARE;
ALL OTHERS, CHARLEY ROBINSON

Taunton
BOOKS & VIDEOS

for fellow enthusiasts

First printing: 1995
Printed in the United States of America

A FINE WOODWORKING Book

FINE WOODWORKING® is a trademark of The Taunton Press, Inc.,
registered in the U.S. Patent and Trademark Office.

The Taunton Press, 63 South Main Street, PO Box 5506,
Newtown, CT 06470-5506

Library of Congress Cataloging-in-Publication Data

Square, David Shath.
        The veneering book / David Shath Square.
            p.   cm.
        "A Fine Woodworking book"—T.p. verso.
        Includes index.
        ISBN 1-56158-093-7
        1. Marquetry. 2. Veneers and veneering. I. Title.
TT200.S67   1995   95-9794
749'.5—dc20   CIP

To my wife, Penny, for her love, help and patience, and to my daughter Bryn for allowing us to share her joy in life.

ACKNOWLEDGMENTS

I would like to thank the following individuals: George Aitkens, David Brickwood, Michael Gidron (Mercury Vacuum Presses), Mrs. Pat Jones, Darryl Keil (Vacuum Pressing Systems, Inc.), Johanne and Norm Leach, Dr. Frank and Ann Manning, Prof. Jasper McKee (University of Manitoba), Pat and Paul Reid, Dr. Ron Steigerwald and Miriam Fliegel, Mr. and Mrs. Steve Steigerwald, Mr. and Mrs. James A. Richardson and Dr. and Mrs. J.R. Sutherland. Thanks also to Franklin International, GAST, General Paint (Winnipeg), Gougeon Brothers, The Manitoba Arts Council, The Manitoba Crafts Council, Princess Auto and Machinery (Winnipeg) and Wainbee, Ltd. (Winnipeg).

A special thanks to Tom McKenna, who edited the book, and to Helen Albert, associate publisher of Fine Woodworking Books and Videos.

CONTENTS

Introduction   **1**

CHAPTER 1
Veneering Basics   **4**
How veneer is made today   **6**
Tools for cutting and joining veneer   **11**
Three veneering techniques   **12**

CHAPTER 2
Hammer Veneering   **14**
The hammer   **14**
Working with hide glue   **16**
Making and veneering a book box   **20**

CHAPTER 3
Mechanical Veneering   **36**
Homemade clamping devices   **36**
A small box veneered with mechanical presses   **42**
Veneering curves with mechanical presses   **52**

CHAPTER 4
The Vacuum Press   **54**
How does the vacuum press work?   **56**
Building a vacuum press   **56**
An adjustable table to support the press   **65**

CHAPTER 5

Basic Vacuum Veneering   **70**

Preparing the top for veneer   **72**

Veneering in the vacuum press   **75**

Adding the solid-wood edge   **78**

Cutting and veneering the legs   **80**

CHAPTER 6

More Vacuum Veneering   **84**

Veneering the tabletop   **86**

Making the apron   **95**

Cutting and veneering the curved legs   **102**

Assembling the table   **105**

CHAPTER 7

Advanced Vacuum Veneering   **106**

Creating a large bending form   **108**

Laminating a panel with multiple curves   **114**

Veneering a panel with multiple curves   **118**

Making and veneering the curved tabletop   **121**

Laminating curved edges for the base of the table   **124**

Assembling the coffee table   **124**

CHAPTER 8

Other Uses for the Vacuum Press 126

The vacuum press as a clamping system 126

Inlaying in a vacuum 128

Bending a panel without a form 130

Veneering concave and convex substrates 131

A simple holding device 133

CHAPTER 9

Vacuum-Press Maintenance 134

Maintaining the bag 134

Pump maintenance 143

A Gallery of Veneered Furniture 144

Further Reading 159

Index 160

INTRODUCTION

I never thought I would write a book about veneering. I was taught to construct furniture of solid wood. My woodworking career began in the 1970s, when I apprenticed with a cabinetmaker who built furniture of solid wood. The "veneer" word was never mentioned in his workshop because veneered furniture was not in vogue. At that time, most woodworkers were entranced with Scandinavian pieces of solid teak, with clean lines and lack of ornamentation.

Even though he spurned veneer, the cabinetmaker did love a piece of timber with a prominent figure. We spent many happy afternoons scouring lumberyards for the perfect plank of roostertail walnut, quilted maple or swirl cherry. The quality of the timber was consistently good, and the dealers didn't mind if we sorted through the wood piles, as long as we restacked neatly. But as time passed, we spent more time searching for perfect wood specimens and less on furniture making because good timber was becoming scarce.

I was aware of the attractive possibilities offered by veneer, but I continued to shy away from it, even when I opened my own business in 1978. I just couldn't break from my solid-wood background. As a result, I began to search farther afield for solid timber with an interesting figure, or any figure for that matter. I even purchased it sight unseen from mail-order dealers. The shipping costs were staggering, and the quality was okay to poor.

It was my disenchantment with the quality of the hardwood I was purchasing that finally motivated me to learn more about veneering. In 1983, I enrolled in a hammer-veneering course at the Yorkshire Craft School in England. The instructor was a graduate of the furniture program at the Leeds Polytechnic, Leeds, England. This proved a positive learning experience. For the amateur woodworker enthusiastic to learn basic skills, hammer veneering offers distinct advantages. First, the tools required are simple and inexpensive. Second, hammer veneering readily lends itself to small projects that can be completed in a few days. The book box featured in Chapter 2 is a traditional design I constructed in my first attempt at hammer veneering. In the summer of 1985, I enrolled in a course at the Anderson Arts Ranch in Aspen, Colorado, because Wendell Castle had been invited to lecture on veneering. I was impressed with his veneered furniture, which exhibited the elegance and fine craftsmanship of Ruhlmann and Rousseau, both of whom I also admired.

This course encouraged me to take a closer look at mechanical veneering. Unfortunately, large-scale mechanical presses are impractical in a one-man shop. The hulking machines require a cadre of people to operate, often with less-than-perfect results. Moreover, new machines are expensive, and even a homemade one can cost thousands to assemble. For these reasons, in Chapter 3, I have limited my discussion of mechanical presses to those that can be built for a few dollars and are portable enough to be considered practical in a small shop. Chapter 3 includes a plan for a box with a parquetry lid that can be assembled in a few enjoyable evenings.

I also enrolled in other courses during the 1980s, including The Furniture Program at Sheridan College, Canada, and the John Makepeace School for Craftsmen in Wood (now Parnham College), England. I also studied briefly with John Sainsbury of Devon, England, a woodworker, tool designer and writer of numerous books on woodworking techniques.

All of these courses substantially increased my knowledge of veneering, but conventional methods like hammer and mechanical veneering did not suit my specific needs as a furniture maker. Deep down I knew there was a veneer press somewhere that met my stringent requirements. But at the end of all my searching, I remained unsatisfied.

I would probably still be constructing furniture of solid wood today if I hadn't read an article in *Fine Woodworking* (#84) by Gordon Merrick, concerning a vacuum veneer press developed by Darryl Keil of Maine. My initial response was, "This can't possibly work." But I was fascinated by the simplicity and flexibility of the machine: It was relatively inexpensive, user-friendly and lightweight; it could handle flat and curved surfaces and boasted a 100% success rate. I constructed a homemade model for $200 and went into the veneering business in 1990. Vacuum-veneering technology is the focus of this book because it meets or exceeds all the veneering requirements of the small workshop.

Chapters 4 through 9 are devoted entirely to this remarkable machine. In these chapters I explain how to build a homemade press and discuss some of the pros and cons of commercial systems. I also demonstrate how to build and vacuum veneer a simple card table. I build a demilune table to show how to vacuum-form a bent lamination with a single-part form and to illustrate the technique of veneering a curved substrate in the vacuum press. I explain how to construct and veneer panels with multiple curves in the press, and I discuss some exotic yet practical uses for this versatile tool. The last chapter is devoted to maintenance procedures, such as how to patch a tear in the vacuum bag. Throughout the book, I also demonstrate the appropriate glues to use with techniques described.

As a last word, what I like best about the veneer process is that it allows me to work with the most beautiful and rare timbers in the world and not feel guilty about depleting the resource. Forests are renewable if managed intelligently, and slicing for veneer is the most efficient method to harvest them. With the growing impetus of the "green movement" and the increasing need to manage our environment wisely, I think the future for woodworkers lies with veneer, not with solid timber.

CHAPTER 1
Veneering Basics

Veneering allows a craftsman to use beautiful woods economically to create wonderful furniture. The technique has a long and colorful history that can be traced as far back as the ancient Egyptians, who used precious woods and metal inlays to enhance their furniture designs. Veneering has been used by many notable furniture makers over the centuries, including Robert Adam, George Hepplewhite, Thomas Chippendale, Thomas Sheraton and Jacques-Emile Ruhlmann, to create some of the world's most magnificent furniture.

Although veneering has been used with great success over many centuries, most one-of-a-kind furniture makers today still prefer the solid-wood approach to furniture construction. Their disdain for veneer grew from the fact that veneer used to be difficult to work with and often yielded less than perfect results: slicing techniques were imperfect and produced veneers that were thick and hard to work with; glues did not adhere perfectly (the veneer had a tendency to lift up over time); and hammer and mechanical processes of veneering did not lend themselves to veneering curved work or large pieces.

Methods of Producing Veneer

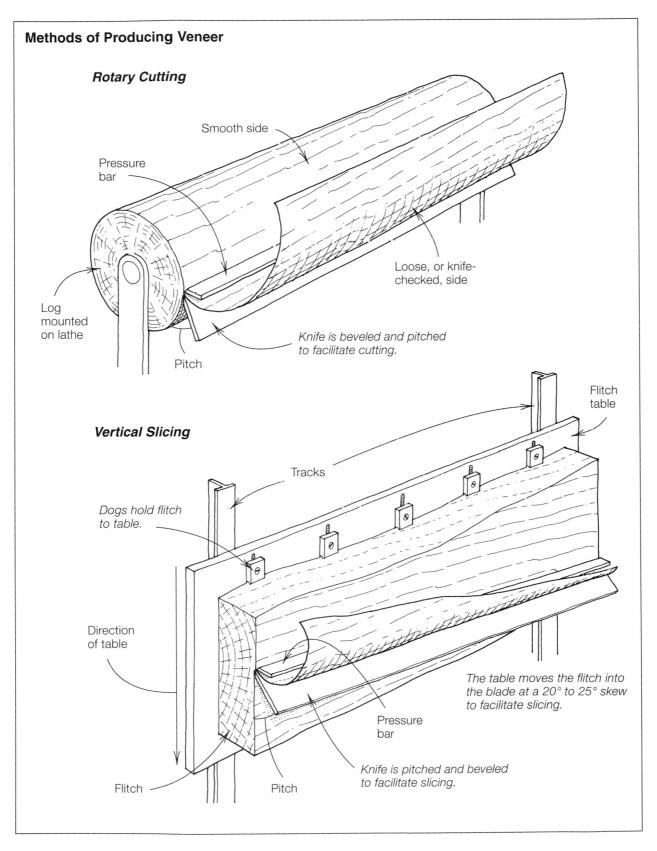

Rotary Cutting

Smooth side

Pressure bar

Log mounted on lathe

Pitch

Loose, or knife-checked, side

Knife is beveled and pitched to facilitate cutting.

Vertical Slicing

Flitch table

Tracks

Dogs hold flitch to table.

Direction of table

Flitch

Pitch

Pressure bar

The table moves the flitch into the blade at a 20° to 25° skew to facilitate slicing.

Knife is pitched and beveled to facilitate slicing.

Fortunately, as we approach the end of the 20th century, interest in veneering among small-shop woodworkers has increased, thanks to advances in veneering technology (such as vacuum veneering), improved slicing techniques and more reliable, user-friendly glues. Unfortunately, the resurgence is also due to diminishing timber resources, especially in the rain forests, which produce some of the most beautiful and desirable species for woodworking. A properly managed forest is a renewable resource, and because slicing for veneer is the most efficient method of harvesting this resource, it seems likely that the direction for woodworkers of the 1990s and beyond will be away from solid-wood construction and toward the more ecologically acceptable technique of veneering. After all, veneering does have a proven track record—some of most beautiful furniture in the world is veneered.

A detailed history of veneer and veneering techniques is beyond the scope of this book. But if you wish to delve more deeply into the subject, you might want to have a look at *Marquetry* by Pierre Ramond and *Ruhlmann: Master of Art Deco* by Florence Camard (see Further Reading on p. 159).

How Veneer is Made Today

Modern veneers range in thickness from $\frac{1}{40}$ in. to $\frac{1}{90}$ in., which, because of advanced cutting technology, is considerably thinner than those of the ancient Egyptians, whose hand-cut veneers ranged in thickness from $\frac{1}{4}$ in. to $\frac{1}{2}$ in. Veneers are produced in three ways: they are sawn, rotary-cut or sliced. Though veneer is rarely cut with a saw today, a small amount of sawn veneer is still produced for the furniture-restoration market. However, it can cost up to five times more than rotary-cut or sliced veneer because it takes more time to produce, and there is more wood lost to sawdust.

Most of today's veneers are rotary-cut or sliced. Today, either method produces a thin, uniform sheet of veneer of excellent quality. Flat-sliced veneer is often the best choice for a one-off woodworker who requires control over the design, while rotary-sliced veneer, with its repetitive wallpaper pattern, lends itself to large door skins or mass-produced plywoods. For more on both cutting processes, see *Understanding Wood* by R. Bruce Hoadley (see Further Reading on p. 159).

Rotary-cut veneer is produced by mounting a log on a lathe and peeling off the veneer, as shown in the top drawing on p. 5. Rotary cutting produces a great amount of veneer in a short amount of time.

Sliced veneer is made by vertical or horizontal slicing machines. Slicing produces veneer with a rich figure similar to solid-wood boards that are plain-sawn or quartersawn. In North America, vertical machines arc preferred, while in Europe, horizontal ones are common. Briefly, here's the process:

First, the logs are trimmed so that they can be mounted on the vertical slicer. These cut pieces are called flitches. The flitches are put in vats filled with scalding water, usually for one or more days. The soaking process softens the wood so that it can withstand the impact of the knife and the shock of being bent around the pressure bar during slicing. The soaking time depends on the species—a large, dry rosewood flitch, for example, might take several days to prepare, while a smaller flitch from a less-dense species like walnut would require less time. Soaking also tends to even out the color in the wood because the water dissolves and spreads the natural dye throughout the flitch.

The flitch is pulled from the vat and debarked. Then it's mounted with dogs on the flitch table of a slicer (dogs are spikes hydraulically driven into the flitch). The table is skewed 20° to 25° to the knife, and the knife is beveled and pitched, which facilitate the slicing action (bottom drawing, p. 5). With each pass of the table, the knife is automatically lowered and repositioned for the next cut. A pressure bar controls the uniformity of the cut and minimizes knife checks (tearing of the grain) by compressing the veneer as the flitch is pushed through the knife. The consecutively cut sheets of veneer are stacked in piles of eight (also called a flitch), and the sheets are dried, trimmed and packed for shipping. For more on the slicing process, read the article "Visiting a Veneer Mill" (see Further Reading on p. 159).

Which side is which?

Every sheet of veneer has a smooth side and a loose, or knife-checked, side. Knife checks are rarely a cause for concern; in fact, I know of only two situations where caution is advised: when a sheet of veneer is bent around a sharp curve and when two sheets of veneer are bookmatched. When a sheet of veneer is bent around a sharp curve (see drawing, p. 8), the knife checks will open if the loose side is not the glue face. This will cause cracks in the finish.

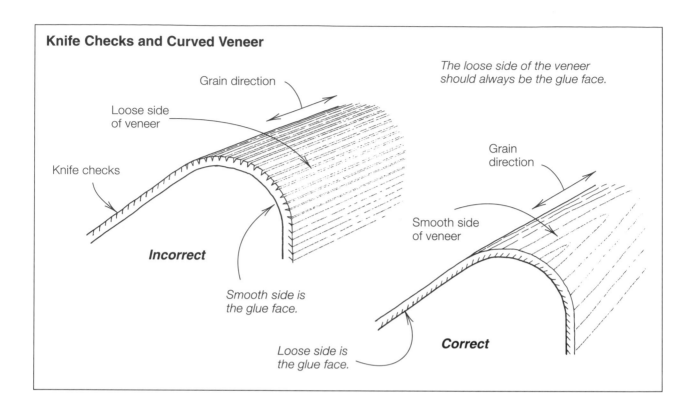

Knife Checks and Curved Veneer

Grain direction

Loose side of veneer

Knife checks

Incorrect

Smooth side is the glue face.

The loose side of the veneer should always be the glue face.

Grain direction

Smooth side of veneer

Loose side is the glue face.

Correct

When two sheets of veneer are book-matched, one sheet must be flipped so that the loose side becomes a finish face. On a blond veneer like white oak that is to be stained, the loose side will absorb more color because it is more porous than the smooth side. When viewed from certain angles, the knife-checked surface will appear slightly darker. This variation in color is extremely difficult to detect in dark veneers that have been stained. If you'll be staining or coloring the veneer and consider the variation in color a problem, slip-match the veneer so that all of the loose sides are glue faces. Slip-matching allows you to stain the veneer without worrying about variation in color.

To discover the loose side of a sheet of veneer, I hold it in my hands and flex it back and forth (left photo, facing page). The loose side will flex outward more easily as the knife checks open. When it is flexed inward, and the checks close, the sheet will feel stiffer. I mark the loose side with a piece of chalk (right photo, facing page). Although I think it is a good idea to find the loose side of veneer, I am not overly concerned with it. In the last 20 years, veneer-slicing technology has improved dramatically, and knife checking has been greatly reduced. Modern slicing machines maintain an optimum distance between the

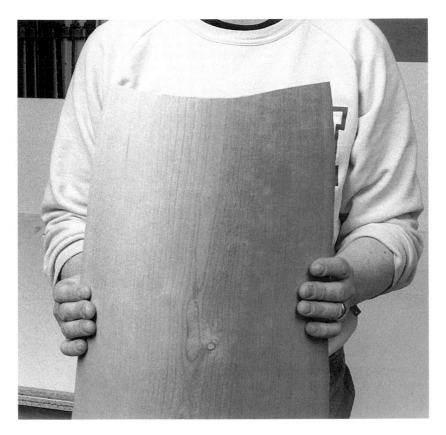

To find the loose side of a sheet of veneer, flex it back and forth (left). The loose side flexes outward easily as the knife checks open. Flexed inward, the sheet will resist bending. Mark the loose side with chalk (above).

knife and the pressure bar. Moreover, because they are sliced to fine tolerances of $\frac{1}{40}$ in. to $\frac{1}{90}$ in., modern veneers are relatively free of tension and bend easily around the pressure bar during slicing. Thicker veneers—$\frac{1}{20}$ in. to $\frac{1}{16}$ in.—are less flexible and release tension by knife checking as they are cut and bent.

Book-match vs. slip-match

There are two commonly used methods to join veneer: book-matching and slip-matching. In a book-match, the sheets of veneer are placed together like the pages of an open book; the first sheet is flipped from the flitch, and the next sheet is slid off the flitch and placed next to the first to match the grain patterns. In a slip-match, the sheets are simply placed side by side as they come off the flitch (see drawing on p. 10).

A book-match is commonly seen on furniture where veneer with a strong figure like swirl mahogany or plume walnut is used. This creates a dramatic visual effect on a cupboard door or tabletop. A slip-match is less dramatic. It is used with bland veneer like unfigured

Book-match vs. Slip-match

The book-match (left) is created by flipping each sheet from the flitch the same way you would turn book pages. Because sheets are stacked in the same order they were cut, the figure can be matched to create a striking look.

The slip-match (right) is created by sliding each sheet off the flitch so that the grain is aligned in the same direction.

maple or birch that looks the same no matter how it is joined. However, as a rule of thumb, remember that a slip-match looks best when an odd number of sheets of veneer are to be joined, while a book-match lends lends itself to an even number of joined sheets.

Sheets in a flitch of veneer are stacked in the same order they are sliced to keep the grain pattern uniform. An eight-sheet flitch allows a cabinetmaker to match the sides and top of a desk or a large table. For this reason, a flitch with a sheet of veneer removed from the middle is less valuable because the interrupted grain pattern makes it difficult to achieve a symmetrical figure on a piece of furniture.

Tools for Cutting and Joining Veneer

Because veneer comes in various lengths and widths, you must develop a reliable technique for cutting and joining the sheets. I experimented with routers and jointers but found that they tear out wavy- or curly-grained veneers. Because most of the veneer I work with is highly figured and because I wasted a lot of time setting up jigs to hold the veneers in position during cutting, I gave up on these methods. By hand, everything went more quickly and accurately, and I soon narrowed the equipment required to the following readily available tools (photo below): scissors, a rotary cutter (a tool from the sewing trade), a utility knife and a good-quality veneer saw for cutting; metal and

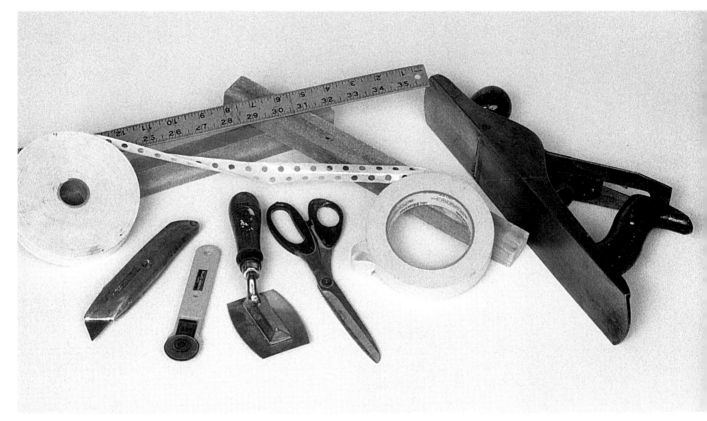

Equipped with this small ensemble of hand tools, you will be able to cut and join any veneer. From left to right: a straightedge, veneer tape, a utility knife, a roller cutter, a veneer saw, scissors, masking tape, an abrasive board and a hand plane.

wood straightedges to guide the knives and the veneer saw; rolls of masking tape and veneer tape to hold the sheets temporarily together; a plane to shoot the edges of straight-grained veneers in preparation for joining; and abrasive boards to shoot the edges of figured veneers (a situation in which a plane will tear out the grain). To make an abrasive board, rip a 12-in. scrap piece of wood to 1 in. by 1 in., then attach 80- or 100-grit garnet paper to the board with spray adhesive.

Three Veneering Techniques

In the following chapters, I explain three veneering techniques: hammer veneering, mechanical veneering and vacuum veneering.

The technique of hammer veneering was used by the Egyptians 4,000 years ago and is still used today. The tools are simple: a hardwood hammer fitted with a brass or aluminum blade to smooth the veneer onto a substrate. The veneer is held in place with hide glue. In Chapter 2, I include a design for a veneer hammer and a book box to demonstrate hammer-veneering techniques.

Mechanical veneer presses use screws or hydraulic force to press a sheet of veneer onto a substrate. In Chapter 3, I describe designs for both types of presses that can be built in your shop, and I recommend glues and substrates to use with mechanical veneering. I also include a design for a box with an inlaid lid to demonstrate veneering with a mechanical press.

Most of this book is devoted to vacuum veneering because it is versatile and relatively easy; it is an exciting new way for a small-shop woodworker to take advantage of the many beautiful, exotic species of wood that are expensive or difficult to obtain as solid timber. The vacuum-bag veneer press, which has revolutionized veneering, is nothing more than a heavy vinyl bag with a pump attached to create a vacuum inside the bag. The veneer and substrate are placed in the bag, and as the vacuum pump removes air from the bag, atmospheric pressure bears down on the veneer, pressing it smoothly and evenly to the substrate. Throughout these chapters, I illustrate some of the many practical—and exotic—uses for a vacuum-veneer press.

Storing Veneer

In a small shop, the most practical way to store long sheets of veneer is to roll them as tightly as possible, stacking each roll inside the next. Then wrap the whole bundle with packing tape—reversed so that the glue does not stick to the veneer (left photo, below). Veneer should be stored at room temperature, kept out of contact with concrete floors, which retain moisture, and kept away from direct sunlight, which will bleach the veneer.

Veneer should contain 6% to 8% moisture when it is applied to a substrate. You should allow newly acquired stock to become acclimated to the conditions in your shop for a few days. The veneer I buy comes from dealers I know and trust, so the quality is guaranteed. If you purchase it from an unfamiliar source, I suggest you check each flitch with a moisture meter before using the veneer. If the moisture content is over 10%, spread the sheets on a flat surface (not on a concrete floor) and allow them to dry in your shop. The moisture content should drop to 6% to 8% within 48 hours, unless the moisture content is excessively high to start. In this case, continue drying until the desired results are achieved.

To prevent a wide sheet from tearing down the long grain, run a strip of masking tape across its width to stabilize it (right photo, below). Smaller sheets of highly figured material, like walnut or imbuya burl, are best stored flat between sheets of melamine (or other sheet material), with a weight on top to prevent curling and warping.

The most efficient way to store veneer is to roll a complete flitch as tightly as possible, stacking one sheet inside another. Then tape the whole bundle together, with the tape reversed (sticky side out).

To stabilize the end of a wide sheet of veneer, run a strip of masking tape across the width. The tape prevents tearing down the long grain during handling and storage.

CHAPTER 2

Hammer Veneering

Hammer veneering was used by the ancient Egyptians, and it was the primary method employed by the 17th-century French *ébénistes* (named so because of their fondness for ebony) to create their veneered masterpieces. It is still in limited use today by hobbyists, furniture restorers and marqueters. Although it is not my favorite technique, hammer veneering is a good way for a beginner to learn about veneering. The tools are simple and inexpensive, and hammer veneering readily lends itself to small projects like jewelry boxes.

The Hammer

The veneer hammer is not really a hammer at all but a tool with a straight metal edge, or blade, that's used to smooth out the veneer on the substrate. I made my hammer from scraps of hardwood and a piece of solid brass cut from an old hinge. If you're going to make your own hammer, make sure the metal blade is nonferrous (solid brass or aluminum) so that it will not react with the water-based glue used to hold down the veneer and cause staining. Also, wood with a high tannin content, such as oak, will react with iron and stain the veneer (top photo, p. 16). Brass-plated hinges are unsuitable because the plating will eventually wear off and expose the steel underneath.

The Veneer Hammer

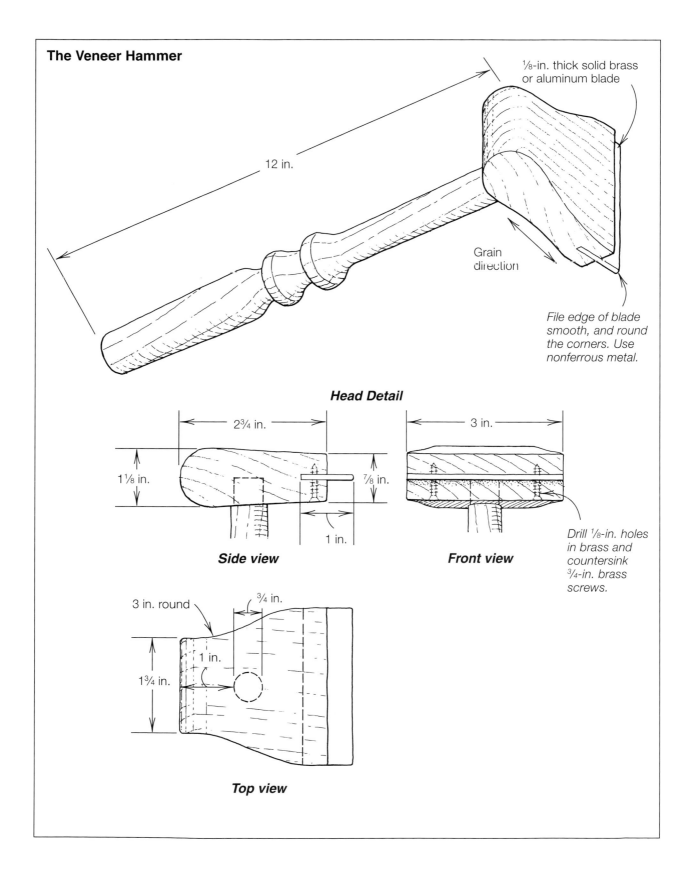

⅛-in. thick solid brass or aluminum blade

12 in.

Grain direction

File edge of blade smooth, and round the corners. Use nonferrous metal.

Head Detail

2¾ in.

1⅛ in.

7⁄8 in.

1 in.

Side view

3 in.

Drill ⅛-in. holes in brass and countersink ¾-in. brass screws.

Front view

3 in. round

¾ in.

1 in.

1¾ in.

Top view

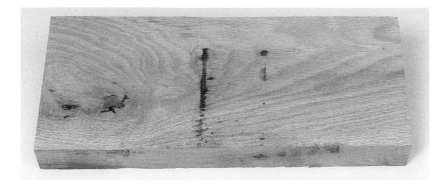

Wood with a high tannin content, such as oak, will react with an iron blade in a veneer hammer to cause black stains on the veneer. Iron will also react with the water-based glue used to hold down the veneer and will cause a similar problem.

If a bubble is found under the veneer after the hide glue has set, it can be worked out by reactivating the glue with an iron and smoothing it with the veneer hammer. Keep the iron set at medium heat (around 140°F to 150°F)—just enough heat to melt the glue without burning it.

The drawing on p. 15 shows a veneer-hammer design. If you own a lathe, you may prefer to turn a handle like mine; otherwise, a square, tapered handle will serve just as well. The dimensions for the various parts of the hammer can be adjusted to your particular veneering style or needs. If you'd rather buy a veneer hammer, check out a large tool-supply house, such as Garrett Wade or Constantine's in New York City and Lee Valley Tools in Ottawa, Canada.

Working with Hide Glue

For centuries, hide glue has been the glue of choice for practitioners of hammer veneering. One of its positive working qualities is that the glue can be reactivated by adding a little moisture to the veneer and applying heat with an iron set on medium, between 140°F and 150°F (bottom photo, above). This is an attractive characteristic for furniture restoration as well as for new work because a bubble trapped under the veneer can be worked out, even if it has been discovered after the glue has set. But don't set the iron temperature too high or leave it on the surface too long, or you'll burn the glue and ruin it.

Hide glue is an animal by-product, although the best-quality glue actually comes from the bones and the sinew, not the hide. The glue is rated according to gram strength, which ranges from 50 to 512; glue with a high number has a shorter open time and greater strength than glue with a low number. Also, glue with high gram strength gels more quickly and is more viscous than glue with a low gram strength. Glue with a medium gram strength is best for hammer veneering.

Hide glue can be purchased in either granular or pearl form. For hammer veneering, I prefer the pearl form because it takes longer to gel than the granular form, which gives me more time to align the veneer. In general, the pearl glue has a lower gram strength, so it's not as strong as the granular glue, but it still has more than sufficient strength to hold down the veneer.

Preparing the glue

To maintain its working quality, hide glue must be kept at a temperature of between 140°F and 150°F. An automatic wire-wound electric glue pot (photo right) holds the glue at the correct working temperature. It takes my glue pot about half an hour to heat a batch. The glue is done when it reaches a consistency similar to hot caramel. A hot plate and a double boiler (photo below) will do the same job for less money. Although less technologically advanced, this system serves almost as well (except when it boils dry). A candy thermometer can be used to check the temperature of the glue. Before you invest hard-earned money in a glue pot, I suggest that you experiment with the double-

An automatic wire-wound electric glue pot (above) keeps the hide glue at the ideal working temperature of 140°F to 150°F. An electric or gas hot plate (left) will do the same job.

boiler system. If you become hooked on hammer veneering, then you can buy the fancy automatic glue pot. A word of caution: Burning hide glue can destroy its working properties, and it really stinks. Moreover, my dog has developed a gourmet's palate for the stuff, and it's more expensive than dog food.

To prepare a batch of glue, pour 2 oz. of pearls, measured by volume, into a plastic container. Then, as recommended by the manufacturer, cover the pearls completely with cold water and allow them to soak for several hours until they become gelatinous. The pearls will easily double in volume in their gelatinous state. Then pour off excess water, pour the mixture into the glue pot and heat it to the appropriate temperature. If the glue is lumpy or thick, add hot water—a little at a time—until a smooth consistency is achieved. If you add too much water to the glue, you'll create too thin a mixture, which will result in improper gelling and working qualities.

It takes experience to estimate the amount of undissolved glue to prepare for a given project because the volume of pearls increases so dramatically when water is added. Also, pearls of different manufacturers expand at various rates. However, excess glue that has cooled can be stored in airtight containers for as long as two months. If the container is not airtight, the glue will only last for about two weeks. In this gelled state, you can judge amounts easier because expansion caused by water absorption has already taken place. In this case, I allow about 1 oz. of glue per sq. ft. of substrate. Never reheat a batch of glue more than four times because it can reduce the glue's strength; for the same reason be careful not to overheat glue.

Testing the consistency of the glue

With the glue ready, the time has arrived to apply veneer to a test piece of substrate. I make a test piece to assess the working quality of the batch of hide glue; a test piece is especially important if you're using a brand-new batch of glue. First brush the glue onto a 6-in. by 12-in. sheet of medium-density fiberboard (MDF), as shown in the top left photo on the facing page. MDF is the substrate of choice for flat surfaces because it is not prone to seasonal movement, the traditional bane of solid-wood substrates.

Once the glue is evenly spread, position a piece of veneer over the substrate, allowing for a generous ⅛-in. overhang on all sides (top right photo, facing page). The overhang gives you more leeway as you position the veneer on the substrate, which can be difficult. The veneer will be trimmed flush to the edge of the substrate with a flush-

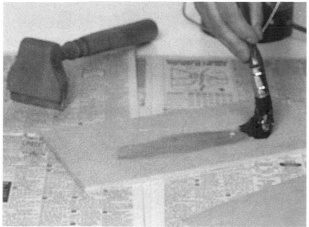

To assess the working quality of a new batch of glue, brush it onto a test piece of MDF (above left) and place a sheet of veneer on it (above). Work from the center of the test piece with the veneer hammer, squeezing excess glue toward the edges (left). If the glue has the correct consistency, a few passes with the hammer should be sufficient.

trim bit in a router. Any attempt to cut a veneered substrate to size on the table saw can result in serious tearout of the veneer, especially on a crosscut.

Working from the middle of the panel, smooth out the veneer with the hammer and squeeze excess glue toward the edges (bottom photo, above). Try not to let the hammer "fall off" the edge of the panel because this can crack the veneer and spread little fractures onto the finished face. If you'd like, you can lubricate the blade with glue to facilitate its glide across the surface. If the glue is of the correct consistency, only a few deft passes with the hammer should be required. You'll be able to tell if the glue batch is bad if the veneer keeps lifting off the substrate in spite of repeated passes with the hammer.

bold figure creates a striking book-match. For contrast, the spine of each cover is veneered with bird's-eye maple. (The box in this example has inside dimensions of 9½ in. by 6½ in. by 1½ in., which will hold a fairly standard-size book. However, because a book box is designed to enclose a specific book, these dimensions can be changed according to your requirements.)

Laying out the book-match

As you remove sheets of veneer from the flitch, number each one in sequence with chalk to ensure that the sheets will remain in the same order they were cut from the log (top photo, below). Lay the sheets of veneer out on a cutting table and arrange them so that the figure is consistent in one direction. For a wood with contrasting figure like Macassar ebony, this is easy; however, when working with wood that has a less defined figure, such as maple, look for a small knot or other reference point to help align the sheets.

As you remove sheets of veneer from the flitch, number each one in sequence with chalk to make sure the sheets remain in the same order they were cut from the log. Doing so makes it easy to arrange the sheets so that the grain is consistent in one direction.

Using a square, draw a cutline on the masking tape across the width of the veneer.

Cut each sheet to length with scissors or a rotary cutter, leaving the masking tape in place because it prevents splitting down the long grain during cutting and joining.

With sheets aligned, establish their length. Each cover of the box is 11 in. long (the covers will be edged on three sides with a ¼-in. piece of solid maple). You need to allow for an ⅛-in. overhang at each end, so add ¼ in. to this measurement. Measure 11¼ in. on the first sheet and mark it with a piece of masking tape that spans the width of the veneer. Position the tape so that you can draw a clearly visible cutline down its center with a square (bottom left photo, facing page). Measure both sheets in this manner, then, with a pair of scissors or a rotary cutter, cut each sheet to length (bottom right photo, facing page). Leave the masking tape in place because it prevents the veneer from splitting down the long grain during cutting and joining. For the same reason, I also tape both ends on the opposite side of each sheet.

Once the veneer sheets have been cut to length, flip over one sheet and hold it against the edge of the other to create the book-match. When placed side by side, the two sheets make a strong visual image that resembles the concentric circles that appear in the water after a stone has been tossed into a pond (photos below). Now you are ready to calculate the width of each sheet of veneer.

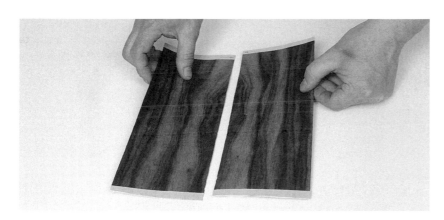

To create a book-match, flip one sheet and hold it against the edge of the other (top). Placed side by side, the book-matched pieces combine to create a strong visual image (bottom).

For the covers of this book box, four 1-in. maple spines are required (one for each veneered surface), so allow for a ⅛-in. overhang on only one side of the ebony; the maple spine will include the other ⅛-in. overhang. To maintain symmetry, try to keep book-matched pieces as close as possible in width. The substrate to be covered is a piece of ¼-in. MDF, 7½ in. wide. You'll need two pieces of ebony veneer 3¼ in. wide, with an extra ⅛ in. added to one piece for the overhang, and one 1-in. strip of maple veneer for the spine, with ⅛ in. added for the other overhang. The total width of the veneer comes out to 8¼ in. But before you start cutting sheets to their exact widths, you must prepare them for joining.

Preparing the veneer for joining

The traditional method of joining sheets of veneer is to cut two sheets at a time so that you have mirror-image knife cuts on both sheets. This will provide a good joining surface. Begin by overlapping the sheets by at least ¼ in. I've found that with an overlap of less than ¼ in., the saw falls away from the veneer. Then, using a straightedge for guidance, make the cut with a veneer saw (photo below). (A utility knife or a rotary cutter can be used instead of the saw.) Whatever tool you use, make several light passes to define the kerf before bearing down for the final cut.

The advantage to this traditional method is that if the saw is held at an angle or wanders in the kerf, the "error" is self-correcting because each edge of the cut is the mirror image of the other. In some cases, a naturally ragged edge or one that's been badly torn during shipping will have to be straightened with a preliminary cut before the join can be accomplished. Just place a straightedge over the ragged end or edge and cut it off with a utility knife.

To prepare a good edge to join two sheets of veneer, overlap them by about ¼ in. Using a straightedge for guidance, make a few light passes with the veneer saw to define the kerf, then make the final cut.

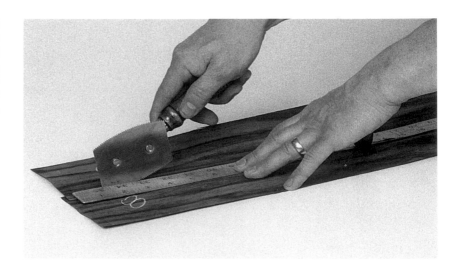

Joining the veneer sheets

With all the sheets cut to width, pull them tightly together with veneer tape. Traditionally, veneer tape is applied to the glue side of the veneer along the length of the joint; perforations in the tape ostensibly allow the adhesive to make contact with the veneer, although some tapes are not perforated. I am mistrustful of veneer tape applied in this manner because the veneer tends to lift from the substrate and is especially prone to chipping at the seams when a veneered panel is cross-cut. And because the tape must be moistened like a stamp, it can cause the sheets of veneer to expand and overlap, thus ruining the joint.

To overcome these problems, I devised a method of joining that uses masking tape and a limited amount of veneer tape applied to the outside face of the veneer. First, establish the glue side of the veneer and turn it upward. Then, starting in the middle, work toward either end of the joint, pulling the sheets tightly together with bits of masking tape (left photo, below). When the joints fit snugly, flip the sheets and repeat the process with bits of veneer tape on the finish face, applying just enough moisture with a damp sponge so that the tape will stick without causing the sheets to expand (right photo, below). Before gluing the veneer to the substrate, remove the bits of masking tape (do this carefully because the tape can lift out wood fiber); the veneer tape will remain in place until the veneer has been applied to the

With the glue side of the veneer up, pull the two book-matched sheets tightly together with bits of masking tape. The maple spine is joined to the ebony veneer in the same manner.

With masking tape applied on the glue side, flip the sheets and affix veneer tape to the joint on the finish side. Apply enough moisture to the tape with a damp sponge so that it will stick but not so much that the veneer will expand and ruin the joint.

substrate, and the glue has dried. It is possible to apply veneer tape to the entire length of the joint, but this entails extra work with the scraper later on, and it won't make a superior joint.

Applying veneer to a substrate

To veneer a cover of the book box, brush hide glue on the ¼-in. MDF substrate and place one of the joined sheets of veneer on top. Try to keep a ⅛-in. overhang all around. Work the veneer hammer from the center of the panel, squeezing glue toward the outside edges (left photo, below). A fair amount of pressure is required, especially if too much glue has been applied, but the veneer should adhere after a few passes of the hammer if the glue is of the proper consistency. Veneer only one side of the MDF for now.

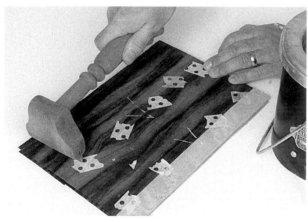

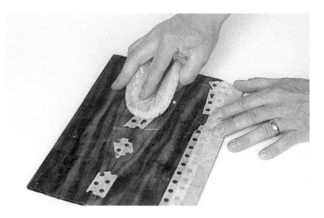

Squeeze excess glue toward the outside edges from the center of the cover. The veneer should adhere to the substrate after a few passes of the hammer.

To remove the veneer tape from the finished side, dampen it with a sponge after the hide glue has completely dried (top). Then shear away the tape with a cabinet scraper (bottom). It may take several light wettings to remove all the tape.

Once the glue has properly cured overnight, remove the veneer tape. However, on a stressed joint like a chair leg, it is always best to be cautious and allow several days for proper curing. In this case, because there is no stress, overnight drying is sufficient. First, lightly dampen the tape with a sponge and then shear it away with a cabinet scraper (right photos, facing page).

Before veneering the opposite side of the panel, trim the overhang with a flush-trim bit in a router (drawing below). To avoid tearing out the end grain of the veneer, trim the long-grain overhang first (begin-

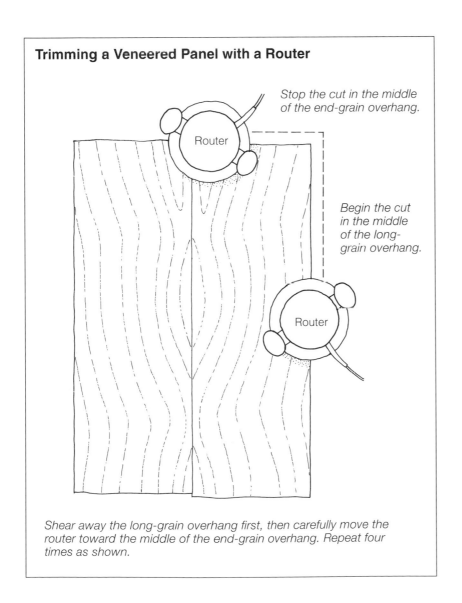

Trimming a Veneered Panel with a Router

Stop the cut in the middle of the end-grain overhang.

Router

Begin the cut in the middle of the long-grain overhang.

Router

Shear away the long-grain overhang first, then carefully move the router toward the middle of the end-grain overhang. Repeat four times as shown.

ning in the middle), then carefully move the router toward the middle of the end-grain overhang. Stop the cut in the middle of the end grain and repeat the steps for all sides. I veneer one side at a time because it is impossible to remove the overhang with a flush-trim bit on a thin substrate if two sides are veneered, and both overhangs are intact: The overhang on one side interferes with the pilot on the bit.

Preparing for the inlay

Once both book-box covers have been veneered front and back, you can prepare to inlay a decorative banding in the top of the front cover. In this case, a length of purchased material is being used, though it is perfectly acceptable to cut strips of a contrasting veneer and use them as the inlay. The substrate is a stable material (MDF), so grain direction is not a concern. But with a solid-wood base, it is important that the veneer be applied in the correct orientation; otherwise, it will crack or work itself loose over time as a result of seasonal movement of the wood (drawing facing page).

First, determine the position of the inlay on the cover, mark it with light pencil lines, then cut the strips to length with a utility knife and a square (left photo, below). The design of this banding does not lend itself to a 45° corner miter, so I cut it at 90° to ensure that all the triangles remain intact. Hold the first strip of inlay in position on the box and cut a kerf around it with the knife (right photo, below), being careful not to mar the veneer by overshooting at the corners.

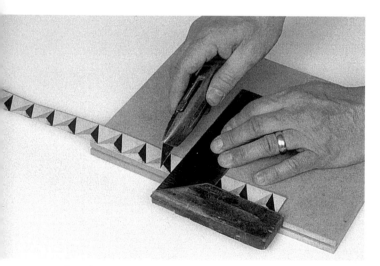

Cut the banding at 90°, using a square for guidance. The triangles are left intact.

Cut a kerf around the banding with the knife, being careful not to overshoot at the corners.

Veneer Orientation on a Solid-Wood Substrate

Example 1 *Correct. Veneer grain runs in same direction as substrate grain.*

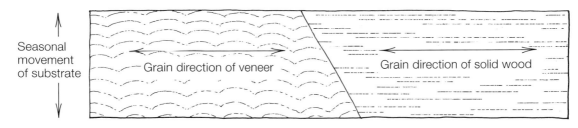

Seasonal movement of substrate

Grain direction of veneer

Grain direction of solid wood

Example 2 *Correct. Veneer grain is 45° to substrate grain.*

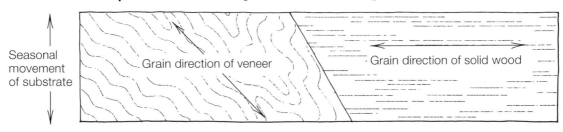

Seasonal movement of substrate

Grain direction of veneer

Grain direction of solid wood

Example 3 *Incorrect. Veneer grain is more than 45° to substrate grain.*

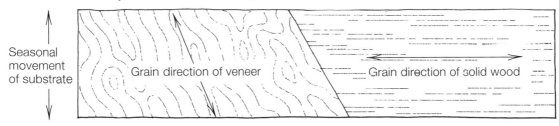

Seasonal movement of substrate

Grain direction of veneer

Grain direction of solid wood

Example 4 *Incorrect. Veneer grain is 90° to substrate grain.*

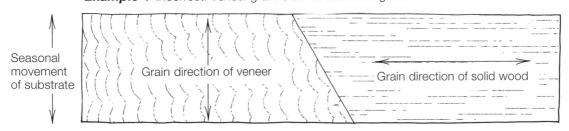

Seasonal movement of substrate

Grain direction of veneer

Grain direction of solid wood

Veneer will not remain stuck to a solid-wood substrate if it is applied to the substrate as in examples 3 and 4 because seasonal movement of the wood is in opposition to the seasonal movement of the veneer. Eventually, the veneer in examples 3 and 4 will crack or come loose. Examples 1 and 2 show the correct alignment.

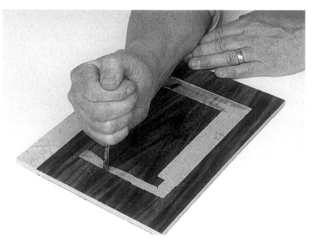

Working to within 1/32 in. of the knife cut, use a router with a 1/4-in. straight bit to remove the veneer. Set the depth of cut to remove just the veneer, not the substrate.

Remove the rest of the waste with a palm chisel. Angle the chisel away from the kerf to create a snug fit for the decorative inlay.

Next, chuck a 1/4-in. straight bit in the router and set the depth to remove just the layer of veneer and not any of the substrate material (left photo, above). Work the router freehand to within 1/32 in. of the knife cut and then remove the final waste with a palm chisel, angling it slightly away from the kerf (right photo, above) so that the inlay will drop snugly into the mortise. This technique for inlaying is known as intarsia, and in my experience, it yields perfect results 99% of the time. If there are some gaps, fill them (see sidebar on p. 34).

When all of the strips of inlay fit tightly in the mortise, turn on the glue pot and get ready to stick them permanently in place. If you have done a good job of cutting, it is sometimes difficult to remove the inlay from the dry mortise. Usually it is possible to pry one strip loose with the point of the knife. This must be done carefully for obvious reasons but, thankfully, is almost always successful. If all else fails, use spray adhesive to attach a small block of wood to the inlay, with paper between the block and the inlay, and use it to lift the strip firmly but gently out of the mortise. Any paper or adhesive left on the finished surface can be cleaned up with a cabinet scraper after the inlay is permanently glued in position.

Installing an inlay with a roller

Once you are sure the inlay fits snugly into the mortise, you can prepare to install it permanently. First, brush hide glue into the mortise. It takes experience to judge the correct amount of glue to apply—too little glue can cause a starved joint, while too much will make a mess and might prevent the inlay from seating properly. I try to apply a wet coat to all parts of the mortise without flooding the area. Never put glue directly on the inlay because the high water content of the glue will cause the inlay to curl before it can be placed in the mortise.

With the glue applied, position an individual strip of inlay in the appropriate mortise. Then take a rubber roller (also called a brayer) and roll it across the surface until the glue adheres to the inlay (photo below). Roller veneering is a variation on the hammer technique, and it is particularly useful in situations where small bits of inlay need to be pressed quickly in position. I prefer the roller in these situations because if a corner of the inlay is not seated flush with the surface of the veneer, the veneer hammer will catch on this edge and lift the inlay out of the mortise. The roller is less likely to do this because it rolls easily over the surface of the veneer and pushes the inlay down into the mortise, rather than lifting it out. A roller can be purchased at any art store. Veneer rollers are available from suppliers of veneering tools.

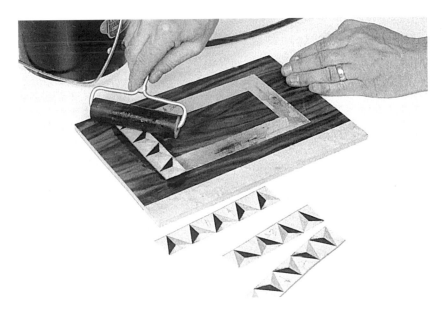

With the inlay seated in the glue-filled mortise, use a roller to press the inlay in place.

A cabinet-scraper holder like this one takes the pain out of long scraping sessions, is easy to adjust and can be pushed or pulled as needed.

With the inlay in place, and the glue properly cured (hide glue can take several days to reach maximum strength), the book box is almost complete. Before final assembly, glue in place the wood trim that frames the front and back panels (see drawing, p. 21) and flush them with the surface of the veneer using the cabinet scraper. The scraper is indispensable for leveling the inlay and cleaning up the veneer. With the covers completed, the other parts of the box can be assembled and then finished.

Preparing veneer for finishing

As a woodworker, you more than likely have plenty of experience with wood finishes, and techniques differ from woodworker to woodworker. But even though veneer can be finished with a variety of traditional methods and materials, there are different pitfalls involved in the surface preparation. You must take great care when preparing a veneered surface for finishing because the risk of damaging the veneer is great, and mistakes may not be easy to repair. That's why I recommend using two simple hand tools to prepare veneer for finishing: sandpaper and a cabinet scraper.

The cabinet scraper allows you to remove material efficiently and accurately. I don't recommend using a power sander on veneer because it can remove a great deal of material quickly—you could sand through the veneer to the substrate in a short period of time—especially if a fresh sheet of sandpaper is on the machine. The cabinet scraper slices fine shavings off the surface of the veneer, plus it's inexpensive. (To learn how to sharpen—or hook—a cabinet scraper for veneering, see the drawing on the facing page.) I recently purchased a holder for a scraper blade that takes the pain out of long scraping sessions, and the blade can be adjusted up and down. Cabinet-scraper holders are available from woodworking-supply stores or catalogs.

To prepare the veneer for its final finish, whether it be oil, shellac or lacquer, first make a few light passes with a cabinet scraper to remove excess glue and to clear high spots, then lightly hand-sand the surface smooth. Wet-sanding is okay, but don't flood the surface. For an open-grained veneer, such as Macassar ebony, the pores should be filled before the preparation and finishing processes begin (for more on filling, see the sidebar on p. 34).

Sharpening a Cabinet Scraper for Veneer Work

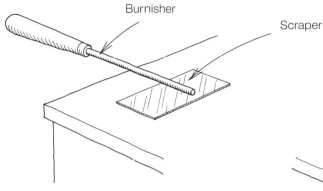

Step 1

Place the cabinet scraper on a flat surface and slide the burnisher back and forth on the scraper to remove a previous hook. Then flip the scraper and repeat. Remember to keep the burnisher flat on the scraper.

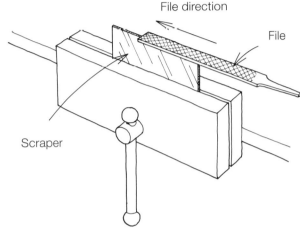

Step 2

Grip the scraper in a vise, and with a fine, flat-mill, square and flatten the edge of the cabinet scraper. File in one direction, not back and forth. Four or five passes should be sufficient.

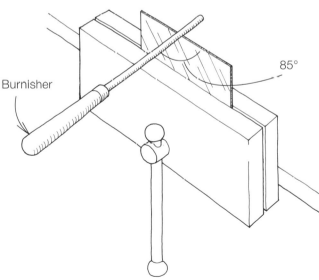

Step 3

Move the burnisher in one direction over the edge of the scraper to create a hook (see detail, right). For soft scraping of veneer, two or three light passes should be sufficient. For heavy scraping, like removing glue from veneer, bear down harder.

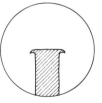

Detail of hook on scraper

Filling Veneer Prior to Finishing

Veneer can be a challenging material to work with, especially when a highly figured wood is chosen for a project. Veneers sliced from burls, crotches and visually exciting exotic rosewood species like tulipwood often have surface blemishes that require filling. Also, some veneers are more difficult to join than others and may result in gaps. These gaps may need to be filled. Inlays, parquetry and marquetry techniques can leave gaps in veneer. These gaps must be filled so that a fine finish can be applied to the piece later on.

I use two basic techniques to fill gaps in veneer. The first uses white or yellow glues, which shrink as they dry; the second uses epoxy. When filling gaps with white or yellow glue, use this marqueter's method: With a veneer saw, scrape a sheet of veneer to produce a coarse dust (left photo, below). Mix a small amount of this dust with the glue, then force the mixture into the gaps. After the glue dries and shrinks, make another mixture, this one using a heavier concentration of dust, and force that into the gaps. Before this mixture dries, sprinkle a final coat of sawdust over the gaps so that the filler stands slightly proud of the surface. When the glue is completely dry, flatten the mixture to the surface with sandpaper first, followed by a light scraping to finish. (Sand the surface first because the scraper's hook could pull the glue and dust mixture out of the gaps.)

I prefer to use five-minute epoxy to fill gaps in veneer because it does not shrink, which means that gaps can be filled in one quick step (right photo, below). Also, the epoxy can be colored with pigments or sawdust to match the veneer. Various metallic-oxide pigments can be purchased from paint dealers to match the color of the veneer. If you're coloring the glue with sawdust, run a matching sheet of veneer under a belt sander to make a fine dust. Then mix that

Scrape a sheet of matching veneer with a veneer saw to produce a coarse dust. Mix the dust in varying consistencies with white or yellow glue until the gaps are filled.

Five-minute epoxy doesn't shrink and can be colored with sawdust or pigments to match the veneer.

dust with the epoxy at a 50:50 ratio; too much glue will give the mixture a transparent look, while too much sawdust will turn the mixture into a thick paste that will not penetrate the gaps. Then follow the same filling procedures as with the previous method: fill, sand and scrape.

Filling pores before finishing

To achieve a reasonable finish on a closed-grain veneer like maple or birch, filling pores before finishing is not absolutely necessary. But highly figured, opened-grain veneers, such as Macassar ebony and sapele, have large pores that must be filled to achieve a fine finish.

There are many brands of paste fillers on the market that will do an adequate job. However, I use white pore filler because it can be colored to match any veneer. I use Japan colors, but earth pigments also can be used. If you must speed drying time, cut the filler with naphtha (although I personally don't rush my finishes); for a slower drying time, dilute the filler with mineral spirits.

To fill pores in a veneer prior to finishing, brush a generous coat of filler onto the veneer, working it into the pores at about 45° to the grain direction (left photo, below).

Allow the filler to dry until it has reached a near-hard consistency (the dry time will depend on what you cut the filler with), then remove the film with a cabinet scraper (right photo, below). Let the filler dry for a minimum of 24 hours before finishing your piece (being a cautious type, I normally wait 48 hours).

Work the filler into the pores of the veneer at about 45° to the grain direction.

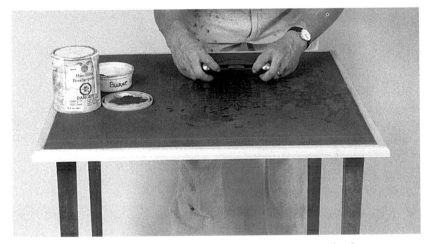

Scrape the veneer with the grain once the filler has reached a near-hard consistency.

CHAPTER 3
Mechanical Veneering

Whoever invented the mechanical veneer press did not have the small shop in mind. I have remained wary of the expensive, hulking beasts, comparing them to unwieldy instruments of torture more suited to a dungeon than a workshop. I seriously believe the reason veneer has remained out of favor with small-shop owners and hobbyists alike is the lack of a suitable method for applying it to the substrate. In this chapter, I discuss do-it-yourself clamping devices and mechanical veneer presses designed for a workshop with limited space and limited financial resources. I show that it is possible to achieve first-rate results with some basic equipment. And once you master the basics and find that you really enjoy veneering, you may want to experiment with resawing your own veneer on a bandsaw from a prized piece of stock. I illustrate my technique of resawing on pp. 40-41.

Homemade Clamping Devices

I once taught a veneering class, and I had a student whose grandfather used a rather unusual technique for veneering large panels. The grandfather placed a veneered panel on his garage floor between two sheets of plywood and then drove his car on top. The student claimed this simple clamping device produced perfect results each and every time.

A Homemade Mechanical Veneer Press

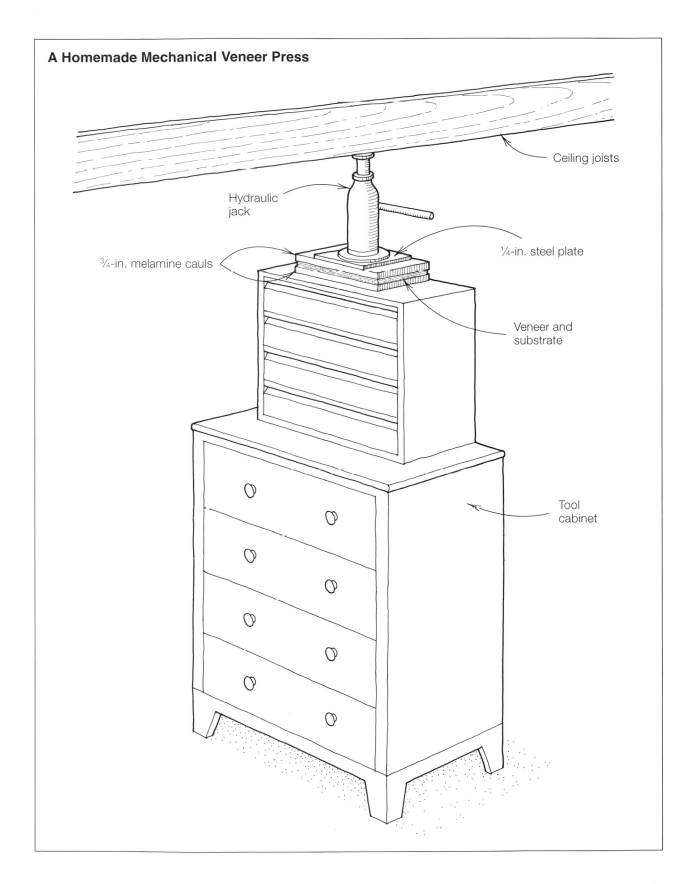

Ceiling joists

Hydraulic jack

¾-in. melamine cauls

¼-in. steel plate

Veneer and substrate

Tool cabinet

Although I don't personally endorse this technique, there is a moral to the story: If a clamping method works, don't knock it, no matter how bizarre it may seem.

The hydraulic press

Years ago, before I could afford to buy handscrews, I used the jack from my pickup to create a hydraulic veneer press. The drawing on p. 37 shows the basic setup. It looks crazy, but it worked well, and I have since modified the design (see the new press in use on p. 45).

A hydraulic veneer press has a few advantages over a handscrew press: A hydraulic bottle jack is inexpensive (a one-ton jack is sufficient), and it can be finely adjusted to apply the correct amount of pressure to the workpiece. Moreover, the jack is quick to operate and less tedious than tightening bolts or clamps on other mechanical devices. The one disadvantage to this setup is that it works well only on small pieces.

The handscrew press

If you own handscrews or other suitable clamps, you can put together the simple press shown in use on p. 46. This setup works well for small panels because uniform pressure can be applied to all areas of the workpiece. For wide panels, however, handscrews cannot apply uniform pressure across the workpiece. So I've come up with a simple variation on the handscrew press: The press shown below is con-

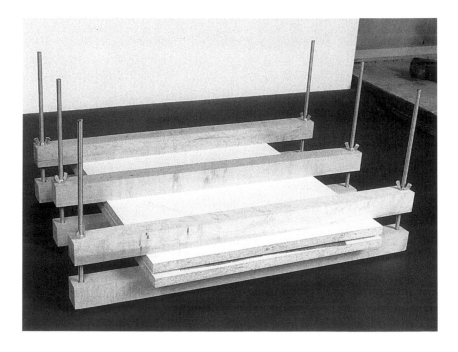

This press is constructed of 2-in. by 2-in. maple crossbearers with ⅜-in. threaded rods that are tightened with wing nuts. The crossbearers have been given a convex profile so that pressure is applied evenly across the workpiece.

Profiling Crossbearers for a Mechanical Press

Straight-cut crossbearers

Straight-cut crossbearers distribute pressure unevenly when pressure is applied to the ends (the middle of the pieces bend upward as in the top drawings). To offset this, use a hand plane to make each crossbearer slightly thinner on its ends. The convex crossbearers distribute pressure evenly across the workpiece (drawings below).

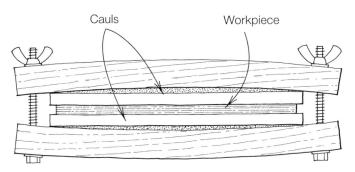

Cauls   Workpiece

Gap is created in the middle when pressure is applied.

Convex crossbearers

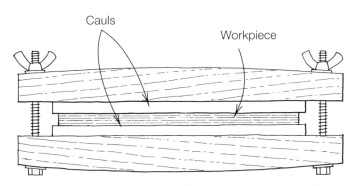

Cauls   Workpiece

No gap is created in the middle when pressure is applied.

structed of 2-in. by 2-in. maple crossbearers top and bottom with ⅜-in. threaded rods tightened and loosened by wing nuts (the wing nuts can be turned with locking pliers if more pressure is required). This particular press is useful for veneering small- to medium-sized panels, but for larger workpieces, the crossbearer size should be increased to 3 in. by 3 in., and the threaded rod to ½ in.

Because wood crossbearers tend to bend upward in the middle as pressure is applied at the outside edges of the press, each crossbearer should be made slightly convex with a hand plane (see drawing above). I use a hand plane for this because I don't want too much of a curve on the piece, and the hand plane gives me more control than a machine would provide. (If it's available, you can use scrap angle iron as crossbearers. The iron won't bow in the middle when clamped, as wood does, and you won't have to shape the crossbearers.)

When I discover a piece of wood with exceptional figure, I sometimes make it go farther by slicing it into veneer myself. This is time-consuming and definitely not conducive to the production of quantities of veneer. Rather, it is an enjoyable way to get the most from a prized piece of hardwood while gaining further basic veneering experience.

Begin by drawing a cutline for the first slice with a marking gauge. Before turning on your bandsaw, make sure the blade is real sharp and that the guides are adjusted properly. I don't use a fence; instead I guide the wood by eye (photo right). A bandsaw never cuts in a straight line: The kerf is always skewed to the left or right of center, which is called blade drift. So when slicing veneer freehand like this, I compensate for blade drift by keeping the stock angled so that I follow the cutline.

However, if you're uncomfortable cutting freehand like this, you can use a single-point fence, which braces the stock but allows you to angle it to adjust for blade drift. If you're resawing a lot of stock, it's probably a good idea to use a rip fence, but you can adust it to allow for drift.

Adjusting the fence angle isn't difficult. Scribe a parallel line near the edge of a square test piece and cut along that line. Stop halfway through the cut, turn off the saw, and pencil a line on the table along the edge of the test piece. Adjust the fence angle so that it's parallel to that line. Make one more test cut to check the angle, make any necessary adjustments, then you're ready to resaw the real stock without worrying about blade drift.

After each cut, run the block of wood (or flitch) through the jointer to prepare a clean face for the next slice (top photo, facing page). If you're cutting freehand or using a single-point fence, you must make another cutline with the marking gauge before cutting another slice; this isn't necessary if you're using a fence that's been adjusted to compensate for blade drift.

It is difficult to slice veneer thinner than $\frac{1}{8}$ in. with my bandsaw, although a newer model with tighter guides might be more precise. If you own a resaw like the Hitachi CB75F or 100F, you will be able to cut wider and thinner sheets of veneer in half the time. The fine cut achieved using either of these machines can eliminate

Guide the wood by eye, following the cutline and adjusting for blade drift. If you're not comfortable with freehand cutting, use a single-point fence or adjust your rip fence to compensate for blade drift.

the need to joint the flitch after each pass through the blade. Whatever machine you use, remember to maintain the order of the pile, as discussed in Chapter 1.

After slicing all of the sheets you can from the flitch, remove kerf marks and give them a uniform thickness. You can use a planer for this job, but first place a piece of 8/4 scrap hardwood over the rollers. This plank serves as a backerboard (bottom photo), which prevents the planer from reducing the veneer sheets to a heap of splinters.

When working with highly figured wood, this may happen anyway, so in this case I don't use a planer. Instead, glue the flat side of veneer to the substrate and then sand to a uniform thickness with a 4-in. belt sander. It is also possible to scrape the veneer to a uniform thickness using a cabinet scraper, but this is very tedious. Those of you with access to a drum sander can avoid all of this work because these machines will produce perfect sheets of veneer with no tearout and no back-breaking labor.

After each cut, run the flitch through a jointer so that there's a clean face for the next slice.

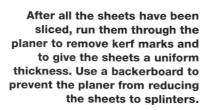

After all the sheets have been sliced, run them through the planer to remove kerf marks and to give the sheets a uniform thickness. Use a backerboard to prevent the planer from reducing the sheets to splinters.

Cauls, glue and substrates for mechanical veneering

I prefer to use ¾-in. melamine for cauls because glue oozing from the veneer/substrate sandwich will not adhere to it. Also, melamine has an absolutely flat, unblemished surface that presses the veneer smooth every time. Melamine is sold at most lumberyards, but it can be costly. I think the cost is worth it because the sheets can be reused. You can use plywood or particleboard as cauls, but be sure to place a sheet of 4-mil polyethylene between the caul and the veneer; otherwise, seeping glue will weld the veneer to the cauls, causing big problems. In general, cauls should be ½ in. larger all around than the workpiece to allow for veneer overhang.

For mechanically veneered projects, I like to use a polyvinyl acetate adhesive (PVA), such as white or yellow glue. PVAs are user-friendly, have a proven track record and are readily available from tool-supply houses or hardware stores.

A Small Box Veneered with Mechanical Presses

When I started my own woodworking business in 1978, I initially generated the best part of my income by constructing boxes of various shapes and sizes. The most popular boxes were those that had been designed with the golden rectangle in mind, meaning that the ratio of width to length is 1:1.618. This ratio occurs in a variety of forms, from the buildings of ancient Greece to modern homes to art masterpieces. The dimensions of the box are based on the dimensions of the golden rectangle: width x 1.618 = length (in this case, 7 in. x 1.618 = 11.326, or 11⁵⁄₁₆ in.). The drawing to the left shows a simple method for laying out the length of a golden rectangle of any given width. Complete construction details for the box are shown on the facing page.

Applying glue to top and bottom panels

I have chosen ¼-in. and ½-in. MDF as the substrates for this project; if you prefer, you can use a wood or plywood substrate, but you'll have to allow for seasonal movement. The sides of the box are also MDF, but it is acceptable to construct them of solid wood, too. The problem of seasonal movement is greatly reduced on the sides because of the narrow width of the pieces required for the side members.

With the ¼-in. panels cut to the specified dimensions, apply glue to the top piece (left photo, p. 44). The easiest way to do this on a small surface is with a cheap bristle brush. As with hide glue, allow 1 oz. of glue per sq. ft. of substrate; a more porous material than MDF may

Laying Out a Golden Rectangle

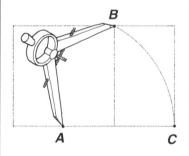

Draw a square and mark the midpoint of one side (A). Stretch a compass from that point to a corner on the opposite side (B). Now swing an arc down to the bottom of the square. The point (C) at which the compass intersects the extension of the bottom line is the length of your rectangle.

A Simple Veneered Box

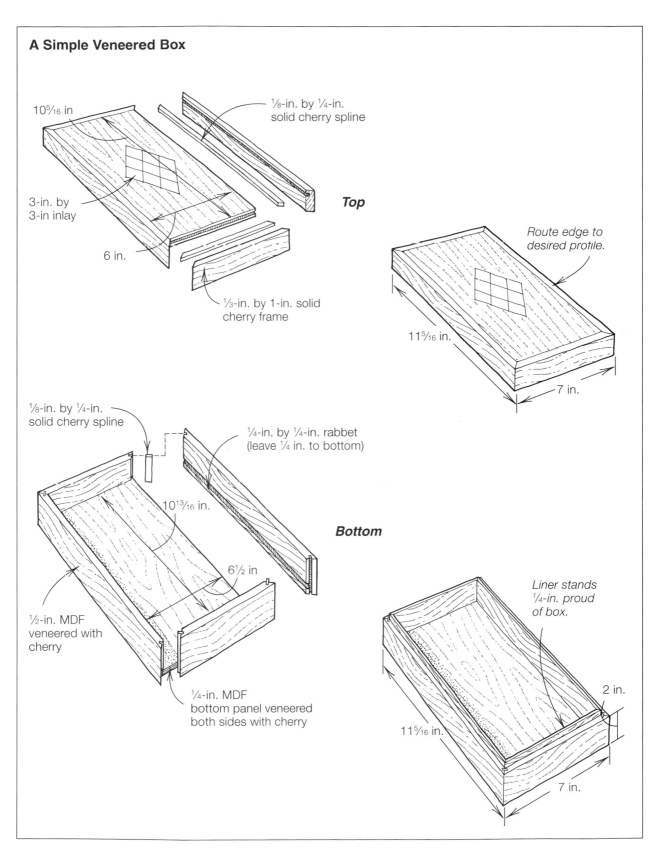

$10^{5}/_{16}$ in

$^{1}/_{8}$-in. by $^{1}/_{4}$-in. solid cherry spline

3-in. by 3-in inlay

6 in.

$^{1}/_{3}$-in. by 1-in. solid cherry frame

Top

Route edge to desired profile.

$11^{5}/_{16}$ in.

7 in.

$^{1}/_{8}$-in. by $^{1}/_{4}$-in. solid cherry spline

$^{1}/_{4}$-in. by $^{1}/_{4}$-in. rabbet (leave $^{1}/_{4}$ in. to bottom)

$10^{13}/_{16}$ in.

Bottom

$6^{1}/_{2}$ in

$^{1}/_{2}$-in. MDF veneered with cherry

$^{1}/_{4}$-in. MDF bottom panel veneered both sides with cherry

Liner stands $^{1}/_{4}$-in. proud of box.

2 in.

$11^{5}/_{16}$ in.

7 in.

Use a cheap bristle brush to apply glue to the MDF substrate, allowing about 1 oz. of glue per sq. ft. on MDF.

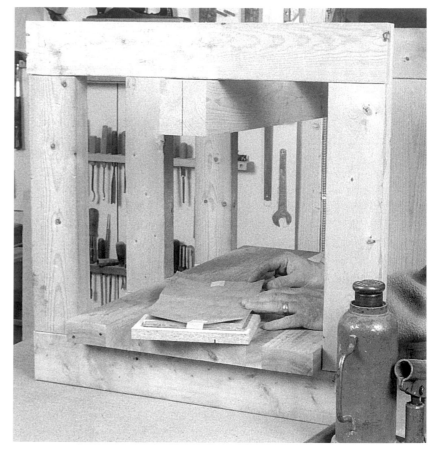

Stick masking tape to the overhang and to the edge of the substrate. The tape will hold the veneer in registration as the panel is pressed.

need more. With the glue applied, position a sheet of cherry veneer on the panel with small pieces of masking tape applied to the overhang and to the edge of the substrate (photo above). The tape holds the veneer in registration while the panel is pressed. For illustration purposes, the panels here have been veneered using both the hydraulic press on the facing page and the handscrew press shown on p. 46.

Pressing the panels

The top piece was veneered in the hydraulic press to demonstrate how quickly it can be adjusted in comparison to screw-operated devices. This particular setup is limited to small panels, but with additional jacks, it could be expanded to include larger workpieces. The top panel is loaded into the hydraulic press, with cauls above and below the workpiece, and pressure is applied (photo facing page).

The handscrew press was used on the bottom panel. On a small panel like this, it is usually possible to span the complete width of the cauls by placing the clamps on both sides of them (photo p. 46). (For a longer and wider panel, you may need to use crossbearers and threaded rods to press the workpiece, as discussed on p. 39.) For longer panels, position the clamps approximately every 6 in. along the length of the cauls to provide even clamping pressure. If the clamps are applied more than 6 in. apart, you won't get sufficient pressure to bond the veneer to the substrate evenly. For small panels, like this one, the clamps can be closer.

It is difficult to explain exactly how much pressure to apply with the handscrews or with the hydraulic press; it will simply take experience. Experiment with a test piece or two before beginning work on the real thing. To find if you've applied correct pressure, look for the following clues after a workpiece is removed from the press:

• If there are bubbles in the veneer and if no glue has seeped through to the surface (on open-grained woods), you have not applied sufficient pressure.

With cauls above and below the workpiece, begin to apply pressure to the panel. The hydraulic press is quick to operate.

The handscrew press does an adequate job of veneering a panel, but it is difficult to set up. In this case, the handscrews are sufficiently wide to distribute pressure evenly to all parts of this workpiece. The clamps are positioned a maximum of 6 in. apart, but on a small panel like this, they can be much closer together.

• If the face of the veneer is completely saturated with glue, you have applied too much pressure, or you've used too much glue. Because of their bumpy nature, it is best to over-tighten a little when pressing burls and other highly figured veneers.

• If the veneer is perfectly flat and smooth, with just a little glue seepage, you have applied the correct amount of pressure.

Remove the panel from the press after three hours drying time. This is the optimum time to allow a white or yellow glue to set at 70°F. Although it may seem excessive, it is better to err to the long side. Any glue should be given 24 hours to cure completely, and for this reason I will not work on a veneered panel until it has sat overnight.

Cleaning up the panels

Shear away the veneer overhang with a flush-trim bit in a router. As mentioned in Chapter 2, the end grain is prone to tearout at the corners, so start in the center of the long-grain side and finish in the center of the end-grain side (see drawing p. 27). Repeat this until all four sides have been trimmed. The trim bit leaves the veneer slightly proud of the edge, so flush it with a scraper and an abrasive board. Work the scraper and the abrasive board the same way you worked the router: from the middle of the long grain to the middle of the end grain.

Assemble the box after veneering

Before scraping the veneered surfaces, add the solid cherry frame to the top panel, as shown in the drawing on p. 43. The bottom panel fits into a ¼-in. rabbet in the sides of the box. The rabbets are cut in the sides after they have been veneered. Before the box is assembled, fill (if necessary) and scrape all veneered pieces for final finishing.

Rip the side panels from ½-in. MDF to the required width, then cut the miter joints on the table saw (photos below). I use splined miters because the splines hold the corners in alignment during clamping and add strength to the joints. The mitered corners also present a smooth

Rip the sides of the box from ½-in. MDF, then cut the miter joints (above). Join the corners with a splined miter (right) for a strong joint and to present a smooth face to the veneer.

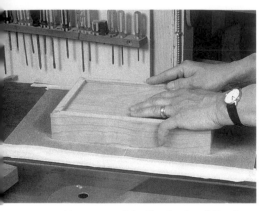

Dry-assemble the body of the box to check for alignment. Then tape 80- or 100-grit sandpaper to the table saw and carefully grind the top edges of the box flat.

face to the veneer; a finger joint or a dovetail could telegraph through the veneer, especially if solid wood is used as a substrate for the sides. Also, finger-jointing the sides would not allow you to veneer the sides prior to assembly.

Although it is possible to veneer the MDF first and then cut the sides to width and length, I prefer to veneer the pieces after they've been cut and after I'm certain they align correctly. If the MDF is veneered before cutting, there's a strong chance that the veneer will chip. The chipping usually occurs on the underside of the kerf and is less likely on a rip than on a crosscut.

The edges of a substrate are normally veneered before assembling a piece, but a box requires a different approach because some adjustment is almost always needed to mate the top with the body. Before applying veneer to the side panels, first dry-assemble the body of the box, mating the bottom with the side panels and the body to the top, to check for alignment. Once you're sure the pieces align and that the top fits the body, veneer the side panels, trim the veneer overhang and then permanently assemble the body of the box.

Then tape 80- or 100-grit sandpaper to the top of the table saw and grind the surfaces flat (photo left), but be careful not to chip the veneer. A plane can be used, but this sanding method works best because it works all surfaces at once and is less likely to chip the veneer.

The strips of veneer are clamped to the top edges of the box. The top corners are mitered; the bottoms are butted.

With the top and the body mated, the edges of the box can be veneered. This can be done with a veneer hammer and hide glue or with PVA or aliphatic glue and clamps, as in the bottom photo on the facing page. (In Chapter 6, I will discuss the use of contact cement for this job.) The strips of veneer should be cut slightly wider than the edges and can be mitered at the corners or butted. For this box, the top edges were mitered, and the bottom ones were butted. Trim the overhangs with a flush-trim bit in the router, and then clean up the edges with a scraper.

If you choose to hinge the box, and the sides are made of MDF, it is good policy to drill holes where the screws will be and then plug them with hardwood to give the screws a firm purchase in the material (for more on this, see pp. 82 and 83). If you decide on a friction-fit lid, as in this example, line the inside of the box with solid cherry (or whatever wood you choose) that stand proud of the body.

Adding a simple parquetry inlay to the top

Parquetry is the art of inlaying geometric designs. One much-used traditional example is latticework comprised of individual squares of veneer arranged to reflect light in different ways. Although a full discussion of parquetry and marquetry (the creation of pictures with inlay) is beyond the scope of this book, I would like to demonstrate a simple latticework to allow the reader to become more familiar with inlaying and to gain further experience cutting veneer. (Should you desire to read more about either technique, I've listed some excellent sources in Further Reading on p. 159.)

Once the frame of the lid has been scraped flush to the veneer, it's time to proceed with the latticework. First, cut 12-in. strips of sapele along the length of the grain with the utility knife (photo below),

Cut 12-in. strips of sapele along the grain. Keep the knife fairly flat to prevent the point from wandering with the grain direction. The 1-in. wide straightedge determines the width of the strips.

Place the metal straightedge 45° to the veneer and use the tip of the knife to cut a clean strip.

keeping the blade as flat as possible to the face of the veneer to prevent the point from wandering with the grain direction. To make things simple, I used a metal straightedge to determine the width of the strips (1 in.). Prepare the end-grain pieces by placing the straightedge 45° to the veneer and, in this case, slicing it with the tip of the knife to ensure a clean cut (photo above); the pattern created by this method is more intriguing than a simple 90° crosscut. Place all of the

Cut the strips again to reduce them to individual squares held together temporarily by the masking tape.

strips side by side, arrange them in alternate rows and attach the strips with thin lengths of masking tape. Then make the final cut (bottom photo, facing page), which reduces them to individual squares held temporarily together by the tape. Assemble these strips in opposite rows, resulting in a checkerboard pattern (photo right).

The preparation for this inlay is similar to that described in Chapter 2, but here a ⅜-in. straight bit is used in the router because this inlay requires a larger mortise in the veneer. Then a palm chisel can be used to remove the rest. Mark the glue side of the inlay (the side without the tape) and the bottom of the mortise with an arrow to indicate the direction the inlay should sit when it is time to glue the inlay in place.

Apply a thin yet adequate coat of white or yellow glue to all areas of the mortise before carefully setting the inlay in position and checking to be sure it is seated properly. Then take the top to the hydraulic press and quickly apply pressure. In this case, a board must be placed under the lid because the cherry edge is already in place. Without the support of this board, the lid would bow under pressure, and the inlay would not seat properly in the mortise.

When the top is removed from the press, the inlay will have masking tape stuck firmly to it. I prefer to use masking tape here instead of veneer tape because to remove veneer tape from an inlay without damaging it, it is often necessary to moisten the tape with water, which raises the grain of the veneer and can soften the glue to the point where pieces of inlay lift out of the mortise. Masking tape, on the other hand, can be easily removed. Wet the tape with paint thinner, let it stand for 10 minutes until the solvent has dissolved the tape's adhesive, then scrape it off carefully.

Paint thinner won't raise grain and has no effect on water-based PVAs and aliphatic glues (for the same reason, it has no effect on veneer tape). Wear rubber gloves at all times when using thinner because it is a petroleum distillate and will irritate the skin. Work in a well-ventilated area, and it's probably a good idea to wear a respirator. Be sure the glue has dried completely and that all the masking tape has been removed before you finish the veneer. It may take several wettings with the thinner and several scrapings to get the surface clean.

Arrange the strips in a checkerboard pattern.

CHAPTER 4
The Vacuum Press

Vacuum presses have been used for years in the aircraft and boat-building industries to form curved panels and structural members. It was not until recently, however, that the vacuum press was adapted to veneering. The system has many advantages over traditional veneering techniques. For the record, allow me the indulgence of restating some of the most pertinent points already made in the introduction: The vacuum press is a versatile, inexpensive, reliable, labor-saving device. To my way of thinking, the vacuum press represents the wave of the future for amateur and professional woodworkers who may have been reluctant to use veneers in the past because of the amount of work involved or because they were trained to build with solid wood.

In this chapter I show how you can make your own vacuum press, and I talk about the equipment you'll need. I also discuss the advantages of buying manufactured presses and equipment. I have included a design for an adjustable table to support the vinyl bag and the platen. There are instructions on how to cut the platen to maximize the effect of the vacuum and a discussion of the most appropriate glues to use with this revolutionary tool for veneering.

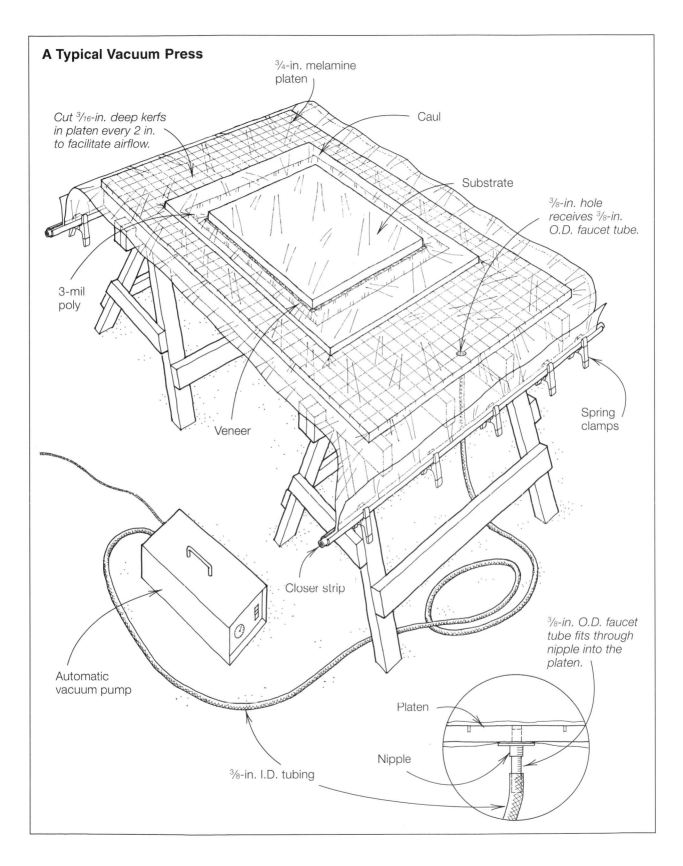

A Typical Vacuum Press

¾-in. melamine platen

Caul

Cut ³/₁₆-in. deep kerfs in platen every 2 in. to facilitate airflow.

Substrate

³/₈-in. hole receives ³/₈-in. O.D. faucet tube.

3-mil poly

Veneer

Spring clamps

Automatic vacuum pump

Closer strip

³/₈-in. O.D. faucet tube fits through nipple into the platen.

Platen

Nipple

³/₈-in. I.D. tubing

How Does the Vacuum Press Work?

A vacuum press is nothing more than a large vinyl bag, with a pump attached to evacuate air from the bag. The platen, which is a piece of sheet material like melamine, is placed inside the bag to support the workpiece and to facilitate airflow (for the basic setup, see the drawing on p. 55). The workpiece is loaded through an opening at the front of the bag, and the bag is sealed tight. The pump removes air from the bag until a vacuum of approximately 25 Hg (inches of mercury) is drawn. When the pressure drops to 21 Hg, a pump equipped with an automatic vacuum switch recycles to bring the pressure back to 25 Hg. If the pump is not equipped with an automatic switch, it will run continuously to maintain the vacuum at approximately 25 Hg. At this point, the atmospheric pressure brought to bear on the workpiece is over 12 lb. per sq. in.—more than enough to press the veneer.

However, clamping pressure is not the main reason why a vacuum press works so well. The secret of the press is its ability to create "intimate contact" between the veneer and the substrate because of constant atmospheric pressure distributed equally to all parts of the workpiece. Moreover, the vacuum draws air out of the wood cells, which is then replaced with glue. Adhesive manufacturers insist that intimate contact and penetration of cellular structure—not clamping pressure—are the two most critical requirements to create an optimum bond between veneer and substrate.

PVAs and aliphatic glues do not dry in a vacuum, but they do "set" because the pump removes enough air and moisture from the bag to let the molecules in these glues form long chains (a process called polymerization). This produces a bond of sufficient strength to join the veneer firmly to the substrate, even though the glue has not completely dried. When the workpiece is removed from the bag, it must be allowed to sit overnight, just as a chair joint must be set aside to dry before it is stressed. Two-part glues that are polymerized by a catalyst are set when the reaction is complete; however, they too should cure overnight to achieve maximum strength.

Building a Vacuum Press

If you are mechanically inclined, you may want to consider building a homemade vacuum press. It will cost less and perform most of the functions of a manufactured unit (for more on manufactured equipment, see the sidebar on p. 66).

Making the bag

The first bag I constructed was of a light vinyl (around 6 mil); it was actually a cheap glazing alternative for storm windows. The bag worked reasonably well to press flat panels but was of insufficient weight for curved work, where it lacked the resilience to return to its original shape (a problem some manufacturers call "memory loss"). Also, the bag punctured easily no matter what shape workpiece I was pressing.

From this, I graduated to 20-mil vinyl. Now I use 30-mil vinyl because of its strength. I buy the vinyl from an upholstery repair shop. To make a bag, first spray the lap joints with acetone and scuff them with 220-grit wet/dry sandpaper (left photo, below). Then spray rubber and vinyl adhesive on the edges of the vinyl (right photo, below) and press the 2-in. lap joints overnight between 2x4s using C-clamps, although I suspect this isn't necessary. (I prefer rubber and vinyl adhesive over PVC cement because of its long open time—30 minutes—and ease of application.) This bag is 50 in. wide and 10 ft. long. It is just wide enough to accept a 4x8 platen for flat pressings (extra joints are required to create a wider bag); the extra foot on both ends is for the closer strips. I had difficulty locating a ⅜-in. I.D. (inside diameter) air-evacuation nipple but finally found one at a pool-supply shop. An

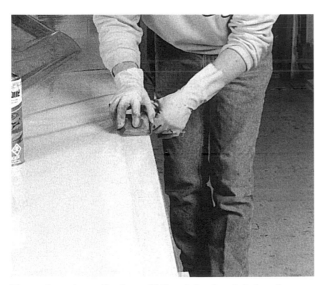

To make a bag, first scuff the 2-in. lap joints of the vinyl with a combination of 220-grit wet/dry paper and acetone to remove the glaze from the vinyl. Wear rubber gloves and a respirator.

With the surface primed, spray adhesive on the lap joints, clamp them between two 2x4s and let the glue set overnight.

easier solution is to check with a manufacturer of vacuum-pressing systems; some sell these nipples individually. Make sure that the nipple is ⅜ in. I.D. and not ¼ in. I.D. because a ¼-in. nipple is too small.

To attach the nipple to the bag, trace a 1¼-in. circle on the bag using a compass and cut it out. Then cut two 4-in. by 4-in. by ¾-in. melamine cauls. In one caul drill a 1¼-in. hole in the center; drill a ⅝-in. hole in the center of the other. Scuff the glue surfaces with 220-grit wet/dry paper and acetone, then apply the adhesive to the bag and to the nipple. Place the caul with the 1¼-in. hole inside the bag, attach the nipple to the outside of the bag and place the other caul over that. Then clamp the sandwich and let it set overnight (drawing below).

I construct my own closer strips from lengths of ½-in. and ¾-in. CPVC pipe. Available at most plumbing-supply houses and home centers, CPVC pipe is more flexible than ordinary PVC pipe. The flexibility of the CPVC pipe makes it easier to close the bag while pressing curved

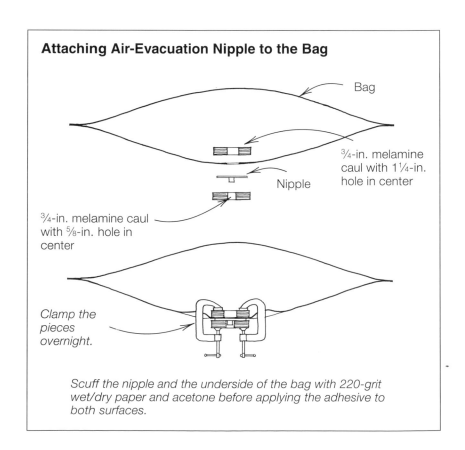

Attaching Air-Evacuation Nipple to the Bag

Bag

¾-in. melamine caul with 1¼-in. hole in center

Nipple

¾-in. melamine caul with ⅝-in. hole in center

Clamp the pieces overnight.

Scuff the nipple and the underside of the bag with 220-grit wet/dry paper and acetone before applying the adhesive to both surfaces.

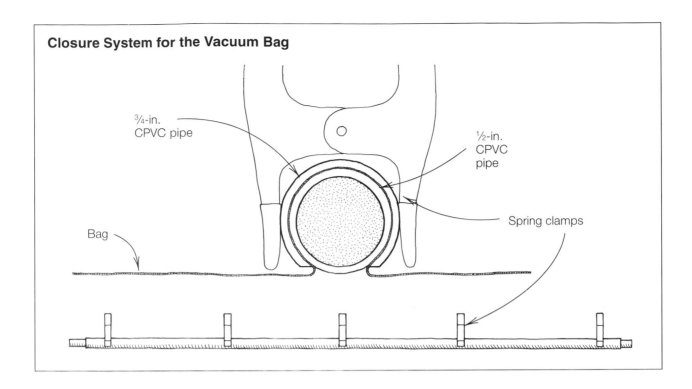

Closure System for the Vacuum Bag

¾-in.
CPVC pipe

½-in.
CPVC
pipe

Spring clamps

Bag

pieces. To make the closer strips, simply cut the ¾-in. pipe on the bandsaw, then clamp it over the ½-in. pipe and the vinyl, as shown in the drawing above. Before cutting up a whole length of CPVC pipe, however, experiment with short lengths to get the best fit for the pipes. When cut, the ¾-in. pipe should roughly resemble the letter C.

Setting up the vacuum pump

The heart of my homemade press is a model 0440-V119 pump manufactured by the GAST Corporation. I purchased it in Canada from a surplus machinery dealer. If you don't want to buy your pump new, you can buy a second-hand vacuum pump from a dealer of surplus or used machinery. Vacuum pumps also can be purchased new from scientific catalogs or from distributors of industrial pumps.

I scavenged a ¼-hp motor from a furnace blower and attached it to the pump with a flexible coupling from the local hardware store. The base is a ¼-in. steel plate I bought for a few dollars at a junkyard.

I recommend using ⅜-in. I.D. flexible vinyl tubing as an air hose. Make sure you choose tubing with an extra-thick wall because light tubing will collapse under vacuum and will restrict airflow. The hose is attached to the nipple with a piece of ⅜-in. O.D. faucet tube cut to length with a hacksaw. The faucet tube fits snugly inside the plastic hose and the nipple and through the ⅜-in. hole in the platen (more on the platen later). It can be easily disconnected from the bag when necessary. To attach the hose to the pump, use a ⅜-in. hose connector with a male thread to match the female thread in the pump inlet. (All of these items are hardware-store staples.) The photo below shows a homemade vacuum press fully assembled.

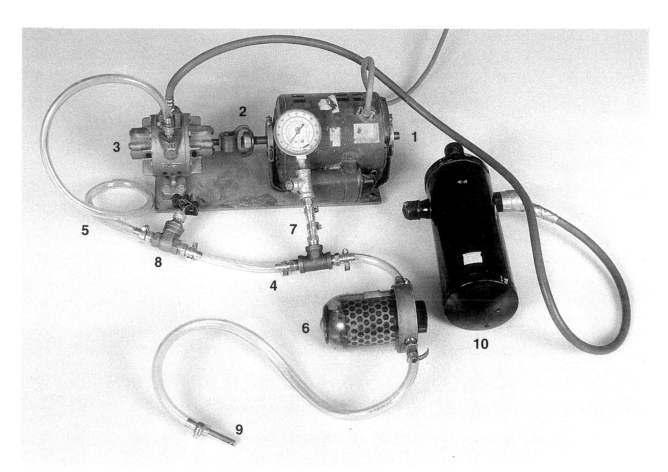

The homemade vacuum press assembled: (1) ¼-hp motor, (2) flexible coupling, (3) 4-cfm pump, (4) ⅜-in. hose connector, (5) ⅜-in. I.D. vinyl tubing, (6) air filter (7) Hg gauge, (8) check valve, (9) faucet tube, (10) silencer.

The pump runs continuously while a workpiece is being pressed, and the noise it generates can be aggravating. Initially, I overcame this by attaching a 50-ft. air hose to the air outlet on the pump and hanging it out the shop window. I am lucky to live in the country, so the neighbors don't complain, but my dog hates it. (If you live in the city or the suburbs, you will probably be unpopular with people and animals.) To solve this problem, you should buy a vacuum silencer (available from vacuum-press manufacturers and machinery dealers). A silencer is an inexpensive investment.

Venturi Pumps

If you own an air compressor, you don't need to buy a vacuum pump to press veneer. You can save money by purchasing a venturi pump, which is a fairly simple device that creates a vacuum by funneling compressed air through a small orifice. Venturi pumps are also manufactured in manual and automatic models, with the latter costing about three times more. In spite of the extra cost, I strongly suggest you buy an automatic unit because it will allow your air compressor to shut down once the vacuum is drawn. Moreover, manual models, for the most part, have a lower cfm rating (as low as 1 cfm) and can take forever to form a vacuum, especially when a curved workpiece is pressed (up to 15 minutes to draw 18 Hg).

I tested the automatic venturi from Vacuum Pressing Systems (the setup is shown below). It has a 3.2-cfm rating and evacuated the air from a 4-ft. by 4-ft. bag with a 3-cu.-ft. form inside in three-and-a-half minutes.

You don't need to buy a vacuum pump if you own an air compressor. You can save some money by buying a venturi pump (upper right in photo). Although not as efficient as a rotary-vane vacuum pump, a venturi pump will get the job done.

The pump for my homemade press has a rating of under 4 cfm, meaning that it evacuates air from the bag at a rate of 4 cu. ft. per minute, but it is adequate to handle most flat pressings. Because of the low cfm rating of the pump, it could take a long time to evacuate all the air from the bag without some help, especially when curved forms are pressed. The bulk of the air can be sucked out with a vacuum cleaner (photo below). This is absolutely necessary when your glue has a short open time. If you're going to be pressing a lot of curved pieces or large pieces, I recommend buying a 5-cfm or greater pump.

My homemade vacuum press served me well when used in a limited capacity. However, once I realized how much I enjoyed working with veneer, it became obvious that I needed to improve my press. I was faced with a dilemma: either buy a commercial press or invest more time and money in my homemade one. I opted to buy a commercial unit because it sported a 30-mil bag, an automatic 5-cfm rotary-vane pump, a vacuum gauge and an air filter, all for under $1,000.

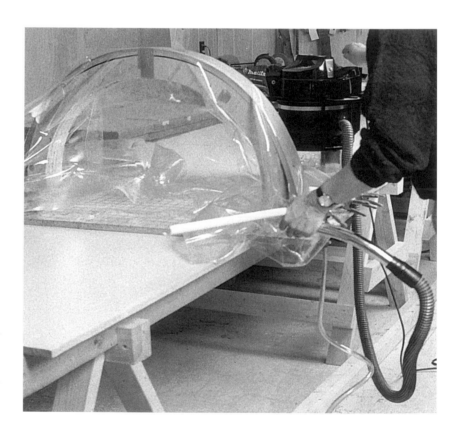

To help a pump with a low cfm rating evacuate air from the bag when a curved form is pressed, exhaust the bulk of the air with a vacuum cleaner first.

Making the platen

Another necessary piece of equipment for vacuum veneering is the platen. The platen is a piece of sheet material with a grid of saw kerfs that provides a solid surface for the workpiece inside the bag. For flat work, the platen can be nearly the full width of the bag's interior, but for tall curved forms, it must be reduced in size to allow the bag to envelop the form. The circumference of a curved form and the platen should be at least 12 in. less than the interior circumference of the bag. That means for curved pressings, you may have to cut down the platen (see p. 101 for a simple method of ensuring that you have enough room in the bag).

The best material to use for a platen is a sheet of $\frac{3}{4}$-in. double-sided melamine because glue does not adhere to its surface, and it is easy to slide in and out of the bag. Vacuum-press manufacturers do not recommend plywood because air trapped in the ply structure can make the pump cycle irregularly and may prevent it from drawing a strong enough vacuum to bond the veneer to the substrate.

To construct a platen, first cut $\frac{1}{8}$-in. wide by $\frac{3}{16}$-in. deep kerfs in the sheet on the table saw. The kerfs are necessary to facilitate air evacuation from the bag. The platen should be kerfed every 2 in. Because the saw must be adjusted in 2-in. increments, it saves time to rotate the sheet clockwise after each kerf so that four cuts are made with one setting of the fence. I make the kerfs a little deeper and considerably closer than recommended because in time they become clogged with glue and other debris. Although I clean them regularly, the extra kerfs and their depth make me confident a vacuum will be drawn quickly and completely. Once the kerfs are cut, remove the sharp edges on the platen with a router or sandpaper so that the edges will not puncture the bag.

Drill a $\frac{3}{8}$-in. air hole 2 in. from the edge of the melamine and centered, as in the drawing on p. 55. Be sure that the hole falls at the intersection of two kerfs so that air will be removed from all parts of the grid. This hole will receive the faucet tube from the air hose connected to the pump. This setup will work with the homemade bag described earlier, but if you have purchased a commercial system, please refer to the instruction manual before you drill—some systems use a tap fitting, while others connect through the top or side of the bag.

Testing the vacuum press

With your vacuum press completed—whether it's a homemade system or one you've purchased—it's time for a test run. In the previous chapter, three test samples were made to determine the right amount of glue and pressure to apply to a substrate in a mechanical press. This process should be repeated for the vacuum press. Because the pressure from a vacuum press is constant and even, you should only be concerned with glue coverage and whether the substrate will swell or react unfavorably in contact with the adhesive. It is always a good idea to do this with an unfamiliar product because it will save grief further down the road.

First cut three 12-in by 12-in. samples of MDF. Place the three pieces side by side and apply yellow glue to all three (photo below). Working from left to right, brush a light coat of glue on the first, a moderate coat on the second, and a heavy coat on the third. The panel with the precise application of glue will show just a little bleed-through, while there will be none on the starved piece and a saturated surface on the sample with an overapplication of glue (photo facing page).

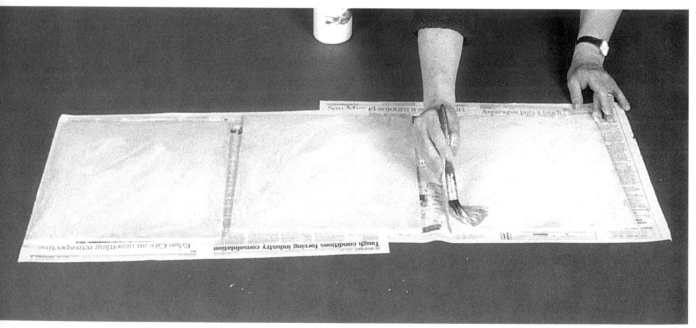

To determine the correct amount of glue to apply to the substrate, prepare three 12-in. by 12-in. test samples. The first piece of MDF is covered with a light coat of glue, the second with a medium coat, and the third with a heavy coat.

The panel with the correct amount of glue (middle) shows just a little bleed-through on the surface of the veneer, while the other two show no bleed-through (left) and saturation (right).

As a rule of thumb, MDF needs about 1 oz. of glue (white, yellow, urea or epoxy) per sq. ft., while particleboard and mahogany plywood require a little more because they are more porous.

Any good-quality woodworking glue can be used for vacuum pressing, but I prefer a two-part urea glue or epoxy (you'll see why as the book progresses), with one exception—I use contact cement for edgebanding (for more on that, see pp. 86-88).

An Adjustable Table to Support the Press

No matter which vacuum system you choose, a solid base will be required to support it. Sawhorses are not normally recommended because the portion of the melamine platen that is not supported sags, which can skew the form or the workpiece or create air pockets, making the pump work overtime. However, I incorporated sawhorses into

Commercial Presses

There are a number of manufacturers of vacuum presses in the United States, although none to my knowledge in Canada as yet. I purchased my system from Vacuum Pressing Systems. (For companies that sell vacuum-press systems and parts, see the list on the facing page.)

There are several things to consider when purchasing a press. The two most important factors are the cfm rating of the pump and the time required to draw a vacuum of approximately 25 Hg. The best systems are equipped with a 5-cfm rotary-vane pump and a ⅜-in. I.D. hose to evacuate the air. These features will allow the pump to draw a flat-press vacuum in 15 seconds. Presses that have a ¼-in. I.D. hose are subject to flow restriction, meaning that the small diameter restricts airflow, and as a result, the press will not perform well.

Yet another important consideration is whether the pump is controlled manually or automatically. A manual pump runs continuously, and as mentioned, the noise can be a real nuisance. Also, the pump and the motor are subjected to more wear and tear and may not last as long as a system that automatically shuts off. (To avoid overheating, do not enclose a continuously running pump in a metal or wood box.)

A plumber's check valve can be installed on a manual pump, which will shut the pump off when a vacuum of 25 Hg is reached. This is fine as long as the bag does not leak. However, if the bag will not hold a vacuum for five minutes, you'll have to open the valve by hand to allow the pump to recycle every five minutes. An automatic pump, on the other hand, shuts off at a level preset at the factory—around 25 Hg—and restarts when the vacuum drops to 21 Hg. The recycling time depends on the condition of the bag and on the effectiveness of the closure system, but a well-sealed press will hold a vacuum for over six hours. The shutoff point on some pumps can be easily adjusted to account for elevations well above sea level (check with the manufacturer to see if this option is available).

Another consideration is the closure system for the bag. I prefer to make my own rod and C-channel closer strips using CPVC pipe and spring clamps (see p. 59). However, you can purchase a similar closure system from the manufacturer.

The next best closure system is a zipper, although zippers are prone to leaks, which cause the pump to work harder than necessary. Small leaks in the closure system or the bag itself are not problematic as long as the system can maintain a vacuum of 21 Hg to 25 Hg. If an automatic pump begins to

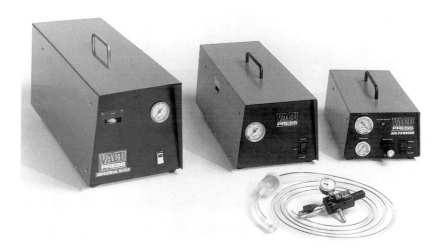

Vacuum Pressing Systems offers three different vacuum pumps. From left to right: the industrial model, the automatic model and the manual model. Photo courtesy of Vacuum Pressing Systems.

recycle every five minutes, manufacturers recommend patching the bag (more on this in Chapter 9). If the bag has been patched to the point where you cannot see the workpiece through the vinyl, you should buy or make a new one.

Avoid bags that are closed with tape because it is a time-consuming process that never results in an adequate seal. And taped bags are usually made of a light, 2-mil film that is good for one pressing only.

A final consideration is the thickness of the bag. I own a 30-mil bag, and it has withstood the rigors of numerous pressings without succumbing to an overabundance of punctures or memory loss, common failings of light-duty bags that lack resiliency. Although 20-mil vinyl bags are common, the heavier 30-mil one will long outlast the thinner bag. In general, a 30-mil bag will cost more that a 20-mil bag (some manufacturers offer an industrial-grade bag).

I have attempted to keep the information in this chapter as current as possible by contacting manufacturers and suppliers of the various products discussed. However, because vacuum veneering is a new and growing technology, I suggest you contact the companies listed below to get the most up-to-date information before you invest in a vacuum system. Most of these companies also sell other veneering tools, as well as accessories for vacuum systems (see photo below).

Manufacturers of vacuum-press systems and parts:

Gougeon Brothers, Inc.
P.O. Box 908
Bay City, Mich. 48707
(517) 684-7286

Mercury Vacuum Presses
P.O. Box 2232
Fort Bragg, Calif. 95437
(800) 995-4506

Quality VAKuum Products, Inc.
43 Bradford St.
Concord, Mass. 01742
(800) 547-5484

Vacuum Pressing Systems, Inc.
553 River Road
Brunswick, Maine 04011
(207) 725-0935

Woodcraft
210 Wood County Industrial Park
P.O. Box 1686
Parkersburg, W. Va. 26102-1686
(800) 225-1153

Woodworker's Supply, Inc.
1108 N. Glenn Road
Casper, Wyo. 82601
(800) 645-9292

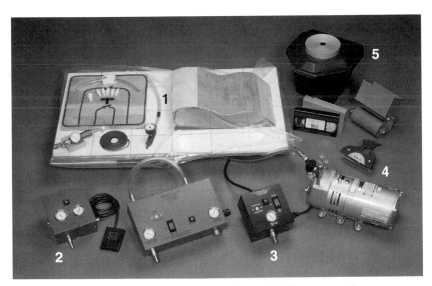

Companies that sell vacuum systems also sell other veneering tools. For example, besides the vacuum-press essentials (1), Quality VAKuum Products, Inc., offers a foot-controlled automatic pump (2), a controller for an electric pump (3), a veneer cutter that's easy on your hands (4) and a glue spreader and storage container (5). Photo courtesy of Quality VAKuum Products, Inc.

the design of a support table that is cheap, stable and quick to assemble; it's perfect for a small, one-person shop. The table is composed of three heavy sawhorses (screwed, not nailed together) with dadoes cut in the top rail to accommodate 2x4 stringers (drawing below). The 2x4s sit on edge like joists to support a melamine sheet on which the bag and the platen rest. I use ¾-in. melamine for the work surface of the table because it is smooth, so it won't catch or puncture the bag, and glue will not adhere to it. You can use another material, such as plywood, but make sure the top side is smooth (AC will work) and free of sharp edges.

An Adjustable 2x4 Base for the Vacuum Press

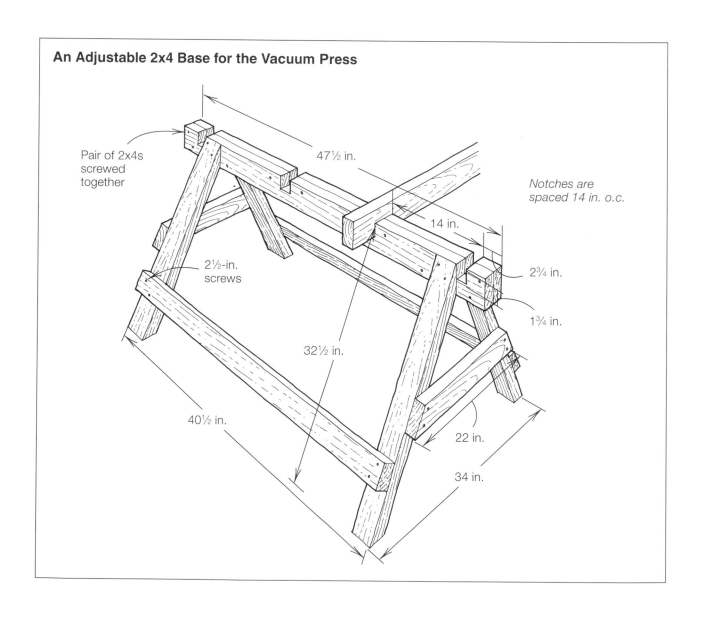

Pair of 2x4s screwed together

47½ in.

Notches are spaced 14 in. o.c.

14 in.

2½-in. screws

2¾ in.

1¾ in.

32½ in.

40½ in.

22 in.

34 in.

In the 8-ft. mode, three sawhorses are pushed together to support four 8-ft. 2x4s and a 4x8 sheet of melamine (above). In the 4-ft. mode, only two sawhorses are required to support the 2x4s and a 4x4 sheet of melamine (right).

The base of the table can be adjusted for different veneering requirements. To increase length, add a sawhorse, place longer 2x4s in the dadoes (top photo, above) and add another sheet of melamine (or a piece of melamine). To decrease size, remove a sawhorse, push together the remaining two and replace the longer 2x4s with shorter ones (bottom photo, above). I usually keep my table in the 4x4 mode because this size handles most of my veneering needs, and it saves space. (The extra sawhorse is handy for other uses, as well.)

CHAPTER 5
Basic Vacuum Veneering

Whether you have built a vacuum press or purchased a commercial one, the time has come to explore the basic veneering techniques that are possible with this reliable tool.

I taught myself to apply veneer with the vacuum press by designing a series of projects that progressed from simple to complex, allowing me to understand and appreciate the versatility of the machine. For this chapter I've chosen a simple project that will demonstrate the basic techniques of vacuum veneering: a card table with an MDF top veneered on both sides with sapele. The tapered oak legs are attached with screw-mount hardware so that they can be removed for storage. I also added a solid-wood edge with biscuit joinery to protect the table from the rigors of the Saturday-night poker game (the edges can also be attached with a spline).

A card table similar to this was the first piece of furniture I vacuum veneered, and at the time, I was grateful to have on hand a sheet of bubinga 30 in. wide by 12 ft. long. This large sheet enabled me to veneer the entire substrate without a single join. If this is your first large vacuum project, you might want to investigate veneers like sapele, bubinga and makore that are sliced from large African species and

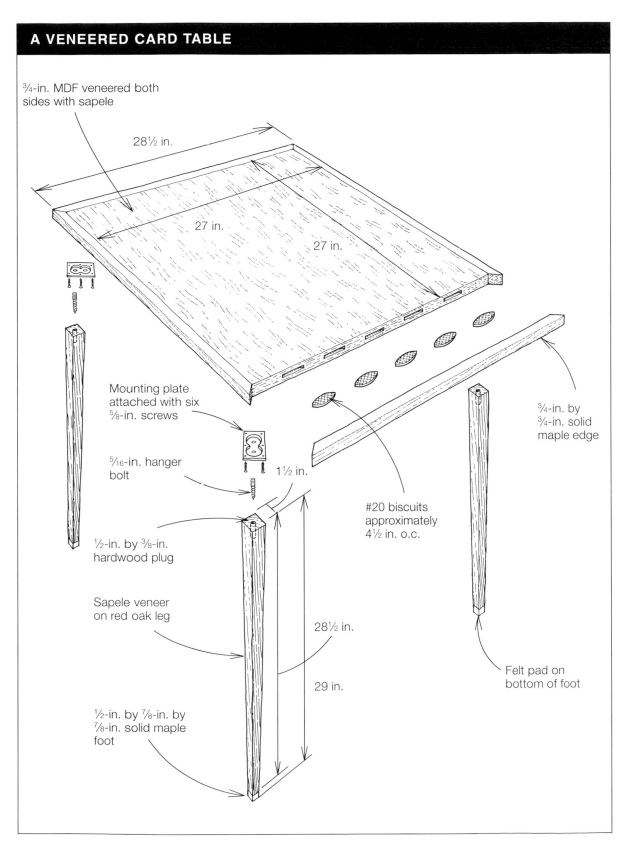

¾-in. MDF veneered both sides with sapele

28½ in.

27 in.

27 in.

Mounting plate attached with six ⅝-in. screws

5/16-in. hanger bolt

1½ in.

½-in. by ⅜-in. hardwood plug

Sapele veneer on red oak leg

½-in. by ⅞-in. by ⅞-in. solid maple foot

28½ in.

29 in.

¾-in. by ¾-in. solid maple edge

#20 biscuits approximately 4½ in. o.c.

Felt pad on bottom of foot

consequently are available in long, wide sheets. These large sheets can turn a first-time veneering job into a painless, joinless experience. The Woodworkers Alliance for Rainforest Protection (WARP) will be able to provide you with a list of lesser-known species that may also be appropriate and have been grown in well-managed forests (consult the Further Reading section for information on how to contact WARP). Construction details for the card table are shown on p. 71.

Preparing the Top for Veneer

Once again I have chosen MDF as a substrate; in this case it's a ¾-in. thick panel. As mentioned earlier, there are many other substrates available, and you may want to experiment with some of them. But if you choose a plywood base, such as mahogany, be sure to glue the veneer 90° to the grain of the plywood. This is how the plywood itself is composed, and cross-gluing will stabilize the veneer, contrary to how the veneer should be aligned on a solid-wood base (see p. 29). The panel is cut to size (27 in. by 27 in.) on the table saw.

After the substrate has been cut to size, apply the glue. White glue is a good choice because it is easy to use, readily available and gives excellent results on small panels with stable veneers like sapele. Measure the glue by volume in a 16-oz. cup, allowing the recommended 1 oz. per sq. ft. of substrate (in this case, 5 oz. to 6 oz.). Pour the glue in the

Pour 5 oz. to 6 oz. of white glue into the middle of the MDF and work it toward the edges with a ¹⁄₁₆-in. notched aluminum trowel.

middle of the panel and work it toward the edges with a $\frac{1}{16}$-in.
notched aluminum trowel (photo facing page), being careful not to let
the glue drool down the sides of the panel because it is difficult to
clean up afterward. Then smooth out the furrows with a 9-in. foam
paint roller (photo above). Do not use a roller with a nap because it
will leave bits of fiber in the glue.

With the glue spread, position the sheet of veneer over the substrate
with the loose side down. Leave a $\frac{3}{8}$-in. overhang all around. The overhang is larger than usual here, but on a large panel, it's a bit more difficult to register the veneer, so give yourself plenty of leeway. To hold
the veneer in registration, affix pieces of masking tape to the middle of
two opposite sides of the panel (photo right). But don't use too much
tape: If the veneer is taped in too many places, it will not flatten evenly
on the substrate during pressing, which could result in the formation
of air pockets underneath.

The sheet of veneer is held
in registration with a few
pieces of masking tape
applied to two opposite
sides of the panel.

If you want to veneer both sides of a panel at once, simply place another caul over the top sheet of veneer. If the caul is not melamine, be
sure to place 4-mil poly between it and the veneer. (Veneering two
sides at once will work only on a thick substrate. If you use a thin substrate, you will find it difficult to trim the overhang because one overhang will interfere with the pilot on the trim bit.) Similarly, if you want
to stack and veneer a number of panels of the same size, put a caul between panels (photo p. 74). This setup distributes pressure evenly to
all parts of each workpiece. If thin cauls are used, such as $\frac{1}{8}$ in. or

When pressing multiple panels of the same size, place a caul between the panels, and 4-mil poly between veneer and the cauls. This setup distributes pressure evenly to all surfaces.

¼ in., they should be cut the same size as the panels because the overhang could be broken off by the force of the vacuum, or the caul could become bowed and prevent an even distribution of pressure (drawing below). I always use ¾-in. melamine for cauls because it can overhang the workpiece ¼ in. without affecting the press. I also like it because glue won't adhere to its surface.

This card table is veneered on both sides with sapele because the table does not have an apron, and it is possible for someone to see the underside without bending too much. However, it is not always practical or necessary to use a high-grade veneer for the underside of a table. Unless a client is particularly fussy, I usually cover the bottom with a backer-grade sheet that is considerably cheaper than high-grade exotics. The backers I prefer are maple and cherry; they are significantly cheaper than exotic sheets of veneer.

Aniline dyes can be used to match the color of the backer veneer to that of the finished-face veneer (top photo, facing page). I prefer aniline dyes because they produce rich colors of remarkable clarity that do not muddy or obscure the figure of a veneer as pigment stains do. Moreover, the colors can be altered, even after the dye has completely dried—this is impossible with a pigment-based stain. Aniline dyes can

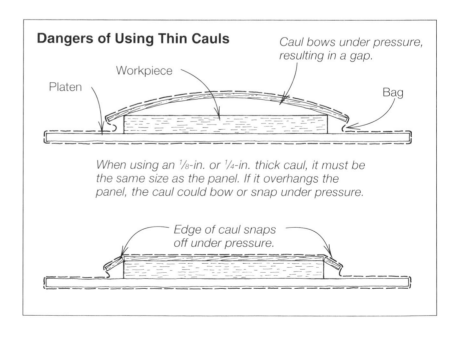

Dangers of Using Thin Cauls

Caul bows under pressure, resulting in a gap.

Workpiece

Platen

Bag

When using an ⅛-in. or ¼-in. thick caul, it must be the same size as the panel. If it overhangs the panel, the caul could bow or snap under pressure.

Edge of caul snaps off under pressure.

be sprayed, brushed or wiped onto a workpiece. Wear rubber gloves when applying them, and a respirator when mixing the powder. To reduce the grain-raising effect of the water, mix the powder in a ratio of 75% water and 25% methyl hydrate (methanol).

Veneering in the Vacuum Press

After many clumsy, anxiety-ridden attempts to load panels into the bag single-handedly, I devised a system to make the procedure simpler and faster. I screwed two elastic cords to my shop ceiling and attached them to both sides of the bag with small spring clamps. The clamps keep the mouth of the bag open (photo below) and are easy to unfasten when the time comes. With the platen already in the bag, place the panel veneer-side down on a ¾-in. melamine caul, which sits on three roller stands aligned with the mouth of the bag. The rollers help when you must load heavy forms or long, wide workpieces into the bag. The caul should be at least 1 in. larger all around than the workpiece so that it completely covers the workpiece. To load the panel, simply roll the caul/veneer/substrate sandwich into the bag, unfasten the spring clamps and snap the closer strip in place. Then turn on the pump to press the panel.

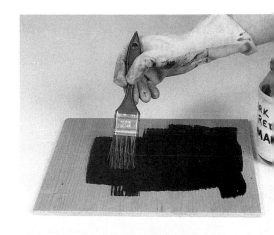

Use aniline dyes to match the color of a backer-grade veneer, like maple or cherry, to the exotic veneer on the finished face.

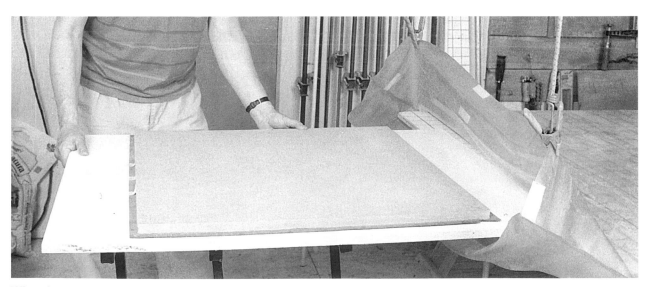

When loading panels into the bag single-handedly, hold the mouth of the bag open with spring clamps attached to elastic cords screwed to the shop ceiling. Place the workpiece veneer-side down on the ¾-in. melamine caul, which is aligned with the mouth of the bag on three roller stands.

Stabilizing Burled Sheets with Two-Ply Veneer

Rippled or buckled burl veneers can be difficult to press. It is a good idea to stabilize them before they are glued to a substrate because they tend to bubble up after pressing. Here's a good way to deal with this problem.

Let's say you're using a burled veneer like imbuya. Take a sheet of backer-grade veneer, like maple, and align it 90° to the grain of the imbuya. Then apply glue to the backer sheet only (top photo). Place the imbuya over the maple (middle photo), and place the two sheets between two ¾-in. melamine cauls (bottom photo) and press the sandwich in the vacuum. This creates a sheet of two-ply veneer. (To prevent curling, keep two-ply veneers lightly weighted between sheets of melamine after they have dried.)

The two-ply veneer can be hand-sanded with a sanding block or run through a drum sander before it is glued to a substrate. Moreover, two-ply veneers do not telegraph bubbles to the finish veneer if there is an area of poor adhesion between the substrate and the glue-face veneer—a rare occurrence, but it does happen.

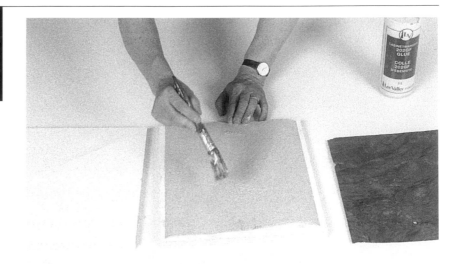

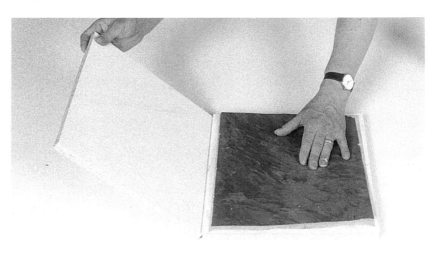

After three hours, remove the panel from the bag. First, check for bubbles and then lightly tap the veneer with your fingertips to find areas that have not adhered to the substrate. With a smooth veneer like sapele, bubbles are very rare. But with a burled veneer like imbuya, they are more common, unless the veneer has been stabilized (see sidebar facing page). However, bubbles can be corrected. Using a utility knife, slice the veneer where it has not adhered or where there's a bubble, then inject adhesive with a glue syringe. Place a small caul over the area and return the panel to the press (see drawing below). It should only take about an hour or so for the glue to set.

After repairing any bubbles, trim each side with a flush-trim bit in the router, then scrape the edge flush with cabinet scraper. To avoid tearout, work from the middle of the long-grain side to the middle of the end-grain side, as explained on p. 27. With one side veneered, flip the panel over and repeat the process. Once both sides have been veneered and trimmed, you can begin to prepare the top for its solid maple edge.

Repairing a Bubble in Veneer

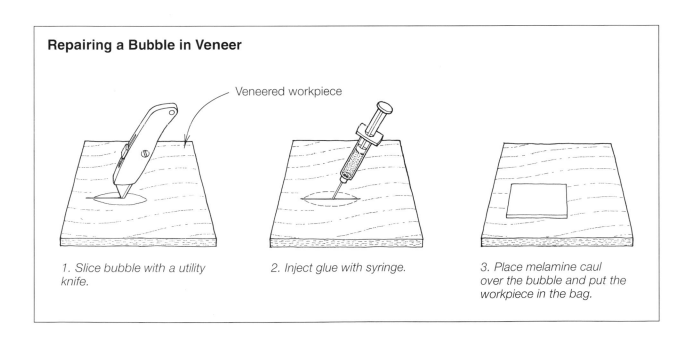

1. Slice bubble with a utility knife.

2. Inject glue with syringe.

3. Place melamine caul over the bubble and put the workpiece in the bag.

Adding the Solid-Wood Edge

This card table has a ¾-in. solid maple edge, which contrasts with the sapele veneer used elsewhere. The maple edges are ripped on the table saw about ⅛ in. wider than the finished thickness of the table-top. The edges are cut 6 in. longer than required so that the gouges at both ends that result from the piece entering and leaving the planer can be cut off. Plane the edges to a width about ¹⁄₁₆ in. wider than the veneered tabletop so that they can be trimmed flush later.

The edges are attached to the tabletop with biscuits. When using a biscuit joiner, it's important that everything be in registration as soon as the adhesive is applied because the biscuits swell in contact with moisture and lock the joint within minutes.

Slot the edges and the panel (photo below), then dry-fit the pieces to check for fit and alignment. Apply glue to the slots, insert the biscuits (top photo, facing page), put the wood edge in place, then clamp the whole thing together (bottom photo, facing page). When the glue has dried, flush up the wood edges to the tabletop using the cabinet scraper.

First, use a biscuit joiner to slot the panel and the maple edge.

After dry-fitting the pieces, put glue in the slots and install the maple edge.

After checking alignment a final time, clamp the edges. An hour's clamping time is probably sufficient for a biscuit-joined assembly.

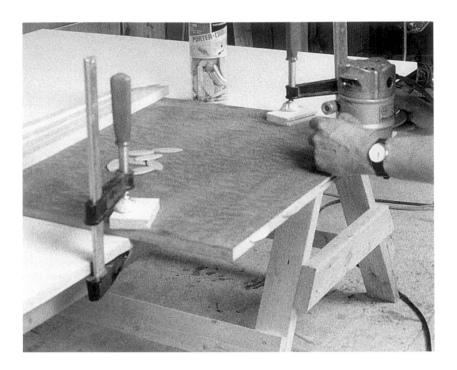

Another alternative is to buy a $^5/_{32}$-in. slot-cutter bit for the router that is compatible with a #20 biscuit and use this as a poor man's biscuit joiner (photo above). This setup is an inexpensive alternative to a biscuit joiner; however, the router must be moved slightly to the right and left of center after it is plunged into the edge to make the slot wide enough to receive the biscuit. After the slots have been cut, dry-fit the pieces to check the alignment, then glue them up (see p. 78).

Cutting and Veneering the Legs

The card table has four 28½-in. long legs, which taper from 1½ in. to ⅞ in. The legs are cut from 8/4 red oak. Red oak is a good wood to apply veneer to because it is strong, takes veneer well and is reasonably priced. (It is also a good wood for use in creating a bent lamination—more on that in Chapter 6.)

To cut the veneer, first make a template out of ¼-in. Masonite that's ½ in. longer and ¼ in. wider than the legs. The template allows for a veneer overhang of ¼ in. top and bottom and ⅛ in. on each side of each leg. Place the template on the veneer sheet and cut the 16 pieces of veneer needed for all the legs, numbering each piece with chalk in the order it is cut to maintain grain direction and symmetry (photo right). The first leg is covered with sheet numbers 1, 2, 3 and 4, the second with numbers 5, 6, 7 and 8, and so on. Apply the even-numbered sheets to the front and back of the legs, and the odd-numbered sheets to the sides.

To apply the veneer, brush glue on the side of one leg (photo below) and position a piece of veneer so that it overhangs the leg on all sides. Hold the veneer in registration top and bottom with masking tape and carefully slide it into the bag on a ¾-in. melamine caul.

The first time I tried this, the veneer moved out of registration, resulting in an ⅛-in. strip of unveneered oak running the length of the leg. Now I stick two extra bits of masking tape at the midpoint of the leg to prevent the veneer from sliding sideways. Once I got the hang of it, I found I could veneer four legs at once in the vacuum press, although I did not attempt a two-sided join, preferring the slow but sure method of veneering one side at a time.

When two opposite sides of a leg have been veneered, remove the bits of masking tape by moistening them with paint thinner, waiting a few minutes for the adhesive to break down, then slicing it away with a

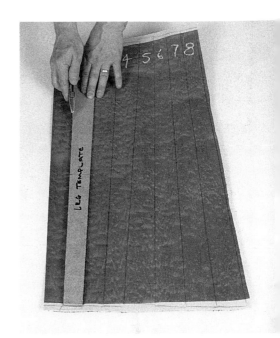

To maintain grain direction and symmetry, lay out the veneer for the legs with the ¼-in. Masonite template, numbering the legs with chalk in the order they are cut. To save time, you can cut through two sheets at once.

Spread white glue evenly with a brush before putting down the veneer. To keep the veneer in registration under vacuum, tape it at the midpoint of the leg, as well as at the top and the bottom.

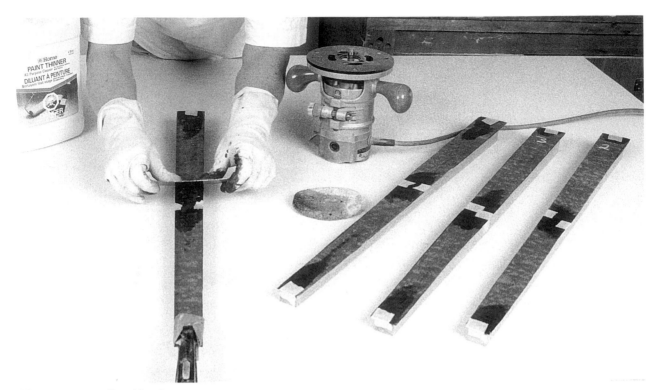

After two opposite sides have been veneered, remove the masking tape using paint thinner and a cabinet scraper.

cabinet scraper (photo above). Do this before you trim the overhang with the router; otherwise, the tape will gum the bit. Trim the overhang on the legs with a flush-trim bit, again working from the middle of the long grain to the middle of the end grain (top photo, facing page). Then make a few light passes with the scraper to remove the overhang left by the bit and finish up with an abrasive board. With two sides done, you're ready to finish up the other sides, repeating these steps. Each leg is capped with a solid maple foot to match the solid maple edge on the top.

Mounting the hardware

With the legs veneered, the hardware can be mounted to the underside of the table. This table features simple, screw-mount equipment because it is inexpensive, easy to find and creates a more stable piece of furniture than traditional hardware. Also, if necessary, the legs can be quickly unscrewed for storage. Although MDF takes a screw well, I prefer to drill ⅜-in. holes and glue long-grain plugs of hardwood into them before screwing the plates into position, as in the bottom photo on the facing page. The plugs provide a solid purchase for the screws. With legs attached, the table is ready for the application of the finish.

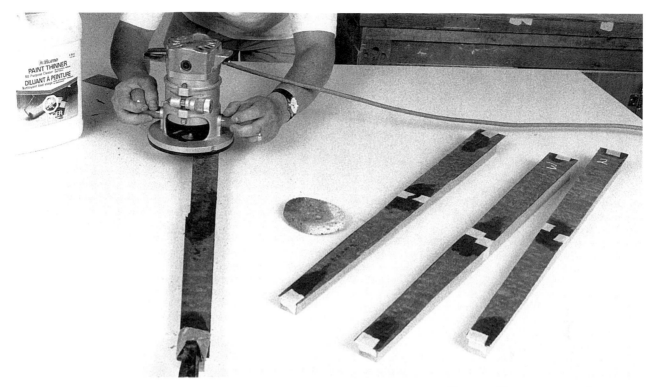

Remove the veneer overhang with a flush-trim bit in the router, working from the middle of the long-grain side to the middle of the end-grain side.

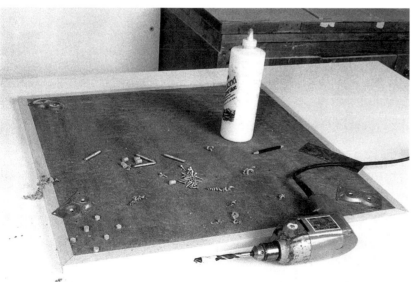

To mount the leg hardware, drill ⅜-in. holes in the underside of the tabletop about ⅝ in. deep and fill them with long-grain hardwood plugs to provide solid holding power for the screws.

CHAPTER 6

More Vacuum Veneering

Once you've mastered the basic vacuum-veneering techniques, you'll probably be eager to pursue more challenging and intriguing projects. I cannot emphasize enough what a simple yet effective tool the vacuum press is when it comes to performing a variety of tasks—not all of which include veneering.

In this chapter, we will build and veneer a demilune table (the finished piece appears on p. 150). This project is a good way to illustrate how to veneer surfaces that are not rectilinear. The table's apron is a bent lamination of red oak, and the gently curved legs, also of oak, are capped with a veneer of walrus-tusk ivory. I will demonstrate how to make the curved apron using a single-part form (anyone who has suffered through the tedious process of building a two-part form will really appreciate this labor-saving method). I will also demonstrate how to cut and join veneer to create a partial sunburst pattern. And I'll explain how to edgeband with contact cement and hide glue, as well as how to laminate the apron and veneer it and the curved legs.

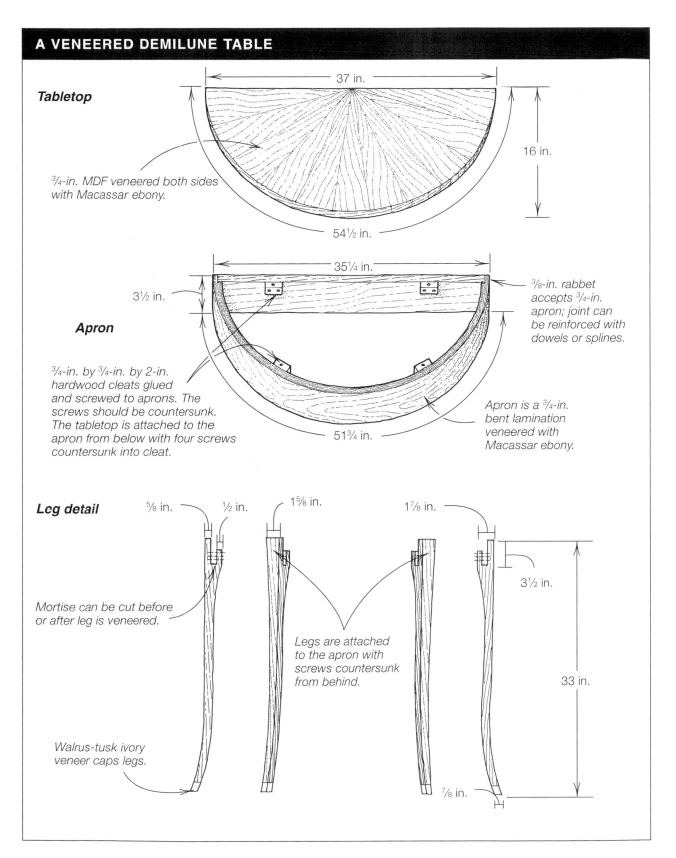

Tabletop

37 in.

16 in.

3/4-in. MDF veneered both sides with Macassar ebony.

54 1/2 in.

Apron

35 1/4 in.

3 1/2 in.

3/8-in. rabbet accepts 3/4-in. apron; joint can be reinforced with dowels or splines.

3/4-in. by 3/4-in. by 2-in. hardwood cleats glued and screwed to aprons. The screws should be countersunk. The tabletop is attached to the apron from below with four screws countersunk into cleat.

Apron is a 3/4-in. bent lamination veneered with Macassar ebony.

51 3/4 in.

Leg detail

5/8 in.

1/2 in.

1 5/8 in.

1 7/8 in.

Mortise can be cut before or after leg is veneered.

Legs are attached to the apron with screws countersunk from behind.

3 1/2 in.

33 in.

Walrus-tusk ivory veneer caps legs.

7/8 in.

Veneering the Tabletop

The demilune tabletop for this example is 37 in. long, 16 in. wide and 33¾ in. high (construction details are shown in the drawing on p. 85). This tabletop is a perfect way to learn how to lay out and veneer a partial sunburst pattern. MDF is the ideal substrate for this type of project because veneer can be applied at any angle without worrying about grain direction. But before beginning work on the sunburst pattern, the tabletop must be edgebanded so that the face veneer will cover the side of the edgebanding.

Veneering the edge: contact cement vs. hide glue

Given a choice, I opt for contact cement over hide glue for edgebanding because edgebandings are difficult to clamp with mechanical or vacuum presses. Contact cement makes the job easier, and I have not experienced a problem with an edgebanding—straight or curved—that has come off because it was applied with contact cement. However, this does not mean that contact cement is appropriate for other veneering applications. I have been told by vacuum-press manufacturers that contact cement will lose its holding power over time on a substrate with a large surface area.

Take a sheet of veneer, in this case Macassar ebony, and cut two strips to cover the front and back edges of the tabletop. Cut the strips 1 in. longer and ⅛ in. wider than the table's edge to allow for overhang (photo below). Veneer the back edge first so that you can cover the end grain of the back piece with the curved edgeband, which is an aesthetic consideration only.

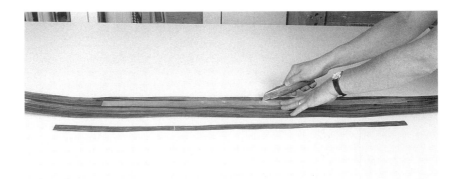

Using a straightedge for guidance, cut strips of veneer for edgebanding that are 1 in. longer and ⅛ in. wider than the table's edge.

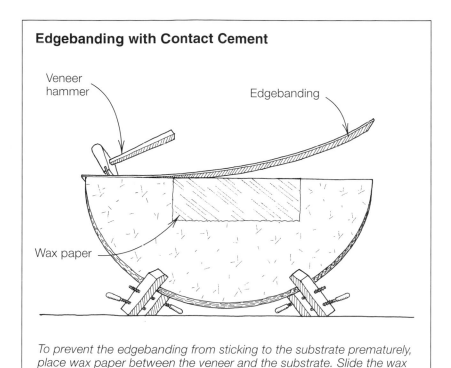

Edgebanding with Contact Cement

Veneer
hammer

Edgebanding

Wax paper

To prevent the edgebanding from sticking to the substrate prematurely, place wax paper between the veneer and the substrate. Slide the wax paper out as you move the hammer across the edgebanding.

With the strips cut, brush contact cement on the loose side of the veneer and on the edge of the panel. Contact cement should be dry to the touch (about 10 minutes) before the edges are veneered. The glue has a fairly long open time of one hour.

Before attaching the veneer, place wax paper along the edge to prevent the veneer from adhering too quickly, before it can be aligned. Work carefully from left to right, pressing down the band with the veneer hammer while gradually moving the wax paper, as shown in the drawing above. Once the banding is completely down, make several passes over it with the veneer hammer to ensure that the edges are firmly glued (top photo, p. 88).

Slice off the end-grain overhang with the utility knife (left photo, p. 88) and flush it with a few light passes of an abrasive board. The long-grain overhang is removed with a laminate-trim bit in the router.

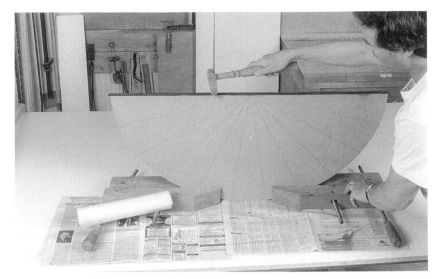

When using contact cement, make several passes over the banding with the veneer hammer to ensure that it is evenly and firmly stuck to the substrate.

After the glue cures, slice off the overhang on the end grain and flush it to the corner with an abrasive board.

Be sure to cant the router slightly away from the panel so that it doesn't dig into the substrate. After routing the overhang, the veneer will still be slightly proud of the substrate, and it should be sanded flush with an abrasive board, as in the photo below.

One reason I don't use hide glue for edgebanding is that it creates a real mess. However, it you insist on a traditional approach, here's the basic technique: Wet the veneer lightly on both sides with a sponge to

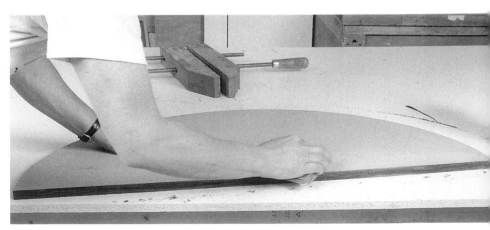

Sand the veneer flush to the substrate with an abrasive board.

establish the direction in which the veneer will bow (top photo, below). I do this whenever I'm edgebanding a curved substrate with veneer and hide glue.

Brush glue onto the concave side of the bow and onto the edge of the substrate (bottom photo, below). Also, lubricate the blade of the veneer hammer by dipping it in the glue pot to increase the speed, or glide, of the blade over the banding. Unfortunately, lubricating the blade like this leaves a messy film on the veneer that must be cleaned off with a cabinet scraper when the glue has dried.

When using hide glue to apply edgebanding, dampen the banding with a sponge to establish the direction it will bow. Make the concave side the glue side.

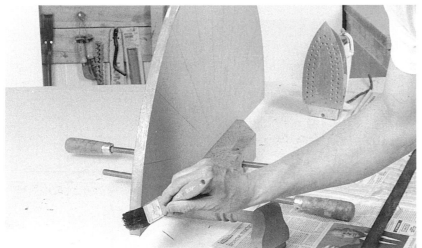

Brush hide glue on the concave side of the banding and on the edge of the substrate. Then run the veneer hammer over the banding until it is firmly attached to the substrate.

Reheat areas of the banding that have not adhered to the substrate to reactivate the hide glue. A few extra passes of the veneer hammer should then be sufficient to stick the banding in place permanently.

Ideally, the entire length of banding should be glued down with a few deft, hard passes of the veneer hammer, with special attention paid to the edges that tend to curl upward. Have a warm iron ready so that areas which have not adhered can be reheated and smoothed with the hammer (photo above). Once the glue has dried, trim the overhang as previously explained.

Laying out a partial sunburst pattern

To make laying out the veneer for the demilune tabletop easier, make a full-size template on a sheet of ¼-in. Masonite. Trace the tabletop's outline onto a sheet of Masonite and, with a marking gauge, scribe a cutline ¾ in. from the outside curve of the tabletop. (If you prefer, you can make your own marking gauge to draw this cutline. For the details, see the drawing on p. 96.) This extra ¾ in. will allow you to veneer the top with a generous overhang. With template drawn on the Masonite, cut it to size on the table saw and then cut the curve on the bandsaw.

The partial sunburst pattern on the tabletop will require you to cut wedges of veneer. When laying out this type of pattern, I try to maximize the yield from whatever size veneer sheets I'm using. In this case, the veneer is 5¼ in. wide, and the circumference of the curve on the layout template is 58 in. I want the wedges to be equal in size, so I divide 58 by 5¼, which comes out roughly to 11. (This is a design consideration only; you may prefer to cut wedges of different sizes; your layout will depend on the width of the veneer you're using and on what you think looks best.) So I divide the demilune template into 11 pieces roughly 5¼ in. wide. It takes some trial and error to lay out the wedges so that all of them are the same size—I do this by eye because I'm not very good with math. I usually make the end wedges slightly wider to compensate for saw cuts and to leave enough for overhang.

When you are satisfied with the layout, cut the template into wedges on the bandsaw and run each one lightly through the jointer to ensure a straight edge. Number each wedge with a pencil and indicate whether it is a piece that will be located to the left or right of the middle so that you don't confuse the order (photo below).

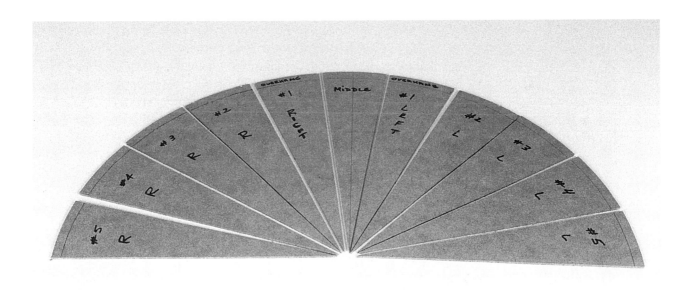

Cut the 11 template wedges on the bandsaw, number them and indicate if the wedge is a left or right piece. Then run each one *lightly* through the jointer to get a straight edge.

Joining veneer to create a sunburst

I experimented with various methods of cutting and joining the individual wedges of ebony veneer for the top—including a disastrous attempt to shoot the brittle edges with a plane and on the jointer—but when all was said and done, I found that a knife and an abrasive board were the best tools for the job (see p. 12 to learn how to make an abrasive board).

Use the wedge templates to cut the individual wedges of ebony veneer (photo below). Because you are working diagonally to the long grain, angle the knife so that the tip of the blade does the cutting. This leaves a clean kerf.

To maintain symmetry of the grain pattern, cut all of the wedges to the right of center from the first sheet of veneer in the flitch, starting with the middle, or center, sheet. Then take the second sheet and cut pieces for all of the wedges to the left of center. Number each wedge with chalk to match the wedge templates and mark the loose side as the glue face.

With the wedges cut and numbered, check the edges for accuracy, working out from the center piece, first to the right, then to the left (top photo, facing page). The knife cut alone can give a near-tight joint if the edge of the template is clean and straight. However, some cleanup is usually required to achieve an absolutely perfect joint. Be-

Place the wedge templates on the sheet and cut pieces of veneer for the demilune top. Because it's a diagonal cut, use the tip of the blade to produce a clean kerf.

With each wedge cut and numbered with chalk to match the template, and the glue side marked, check the edges for accuracy. Work from the center piece out.

cause a plane will tear out a diagonally cut edge, shoot the veneer with an abrasive board instead. To ensure that the edge remains square, place the veneer between sheets of melamine and then sand it.

When all of the joints have been sanded, flip each piece of veneer so that the glue side is up and begin to assemble the wedges with bits of masking tape, using the joining technique discussed in Chapter 2 (see pp. 25-26). With the veneer wedges held together with masking tape, place the substrate over the assembled sheet to check the fit. There should be an overhang of about ⅛ in. at the back of the substrate and a healthy ⅝ in. around the front curve. Once you're sure of the fit, remove the substrate, flip the sheet and apply bits of veneer tape to the finish face of the veneer (photo below). Then remove the masking tape from the glue side. That done, it's time to to press the top.

Once you're sure that the sheet fits the substrate, apply bits of veneer tape to the finish side. Then flip the sheet and remove the masking tape to ensure a good bond between veneer and substrate.

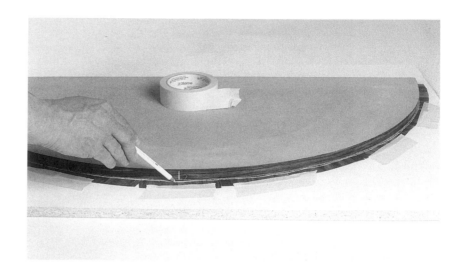

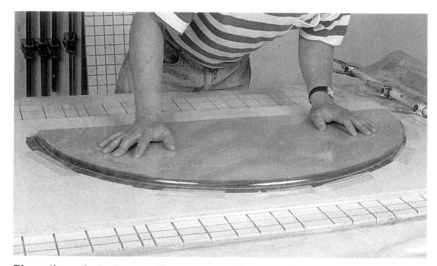

Place the substrate over the veneer and use a white pencil or chalk to trace a line around the substrate (top) to help align the substrate during glue up. The line also allows you to check that the two pieces remain in registration as the vacuum is drawn (bottom).

To hold the assembled sheet of veneer in registration during pressing, place the veneer on the caul so that the glue side is face up. Position the substrate over the veneer, tape the sheet to the caul and trace the substrate with a white pencil or chalk (top photo, above). Then remove the substrate, apply glue as previously described and reposition it using the white line for registration. Then slide the caul carefully into the bag and watch closely as the vacuum forms to be sure that the substrate does not move out of registration (bottom photo, above).

Making the Apron

The table's apron is a ³/₄-in. thick by 3½-in. wide bent lamination constructed of six layers of ⅛-in. red oak veneered with Macassar ebony. The apron provides a good example of how to make a bent lamination in the vacuum press. No matter what species of wood I am bending, I always choose clear stock (no knots or curly grain) because it bends easier and is less prone to cracking. Red oak is a good choice for a bent lamination, but other woods that are good for this purpose include black walnut, maple, white oak, ash, birch and beech.

The six red-oak laminates should be cut ¼ in. wider and 3 in. to 4 in. longer at both ends to allow for bending and trimming. Rip them on the table saw from a piece of 8/4 oak to a thickness of ³/₁₆ in., which will allow you to plane them to remove the saw kerfs. Ideally, the laminates should be glued in the same order they were cut from the flitch so that the lamination will resemble the original board.

Building a two-part form for a bent lamination (photo below) is a tedious, time-consuming process that can test one's patience and skill. One of the many remarkable features of a vacuum press is that it allows a woodworker to create perfect bent laminations with a single-part form that is simple to make (see sidebar p. 96).

A two-part bending form, like the one shown in the photo, is difficult and time-consuming to create. With the vacuum press, a lamination can be bent with a single-part form and no clamps.

To bend the lamination for the demilune table's apron, you first must make a bending form. This single-part form is made of ¾-in. spruce plywood glued and screwed together. Here's how it's made.

Step 1. Establish the circumference of the five laminates of plywood by making a homemade marking gauge out of a wood block, a pencil and a dowel. The marking gauge is used to trace a pencil line inside the circumference of the template (see Step 2). The distance between the dowel and the pencil is equal to the thickness of the apron (¾ in.), plus the thickness of the front block of the leg (⅝ in.), plus the overhang of the tabletop (¼ in.) for a total of 1⅝ in.

Step 2. On the bandsaw, cut a sheet of ¼-in. Masonite to the same dimensions as the demilune tabletop. Use a ¼-in. six-tooth blade, which gives a smooth cut. Then place the marking gauge on the template, trace around its circumference and cut along the pencil line on the bandsaw.

Making a Bending Form

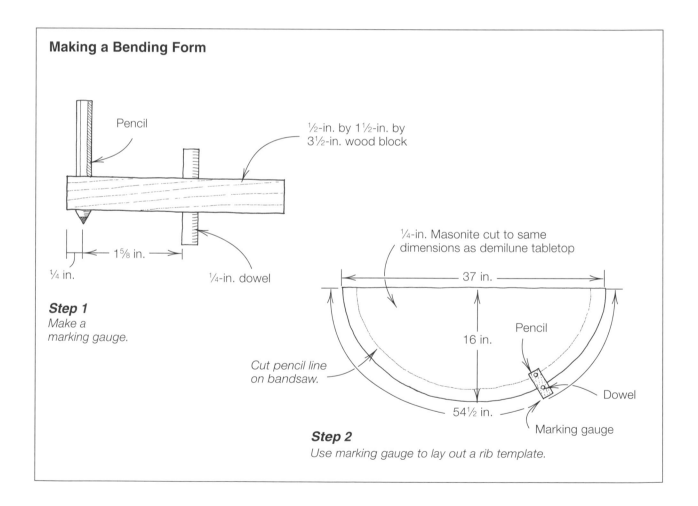

Pencil

½-in. by 1½-in. by 3½-in. wood block

1⅝ in.

¼ in.

¼-in. dowel

Step 1
Make a marking gauge.

¼-in. Masonite cut to same dimensions as demilune tabletop

37 in.

16 in.

Pencil

Cut pencil line on bandsaw.

54½ in.

Dowel

Marking gauge

Step 2
Use marking gauge to lay out a rib template.

Step 3. Cut five pieces of the ¾-in. plywood to 40 in. by 16 in., place the template on one sheet and trace the circumference of the template. To speed cutting and to ensure that all ribs are symmetrical, place the traced template on top and glue and screw the whole pile together with #10 3½-in. screws. Make sure the screws fall within the cutline, and let it set overnight. Then cut the pile on the bandsaw. To lighten the form,

remove the waste on the underside of it. The bag will be drawn into the opening under the form and will prevent it from collapsing—atmospheric pressure is equal in all directions.

Step 4. The laminates are cut about 3 in. to 4 in. longer than their finished lengths to allow for bending and trimming, so you'll need extra room on the bottom of the form. Screw 3-in. or 4-in.

blocks (either hardwood or softwood blocks will work) on both ends of the form. If you prefer, simply make the form extra-long. Strike a line at the center of the form to help later in aligning the laminates with the form. The bending form is the same circumference as the finished apron, but it is ¼ in. wider than the apron to allow the glued lamination to be trimmed with a plane to its finished width of 3½ in.

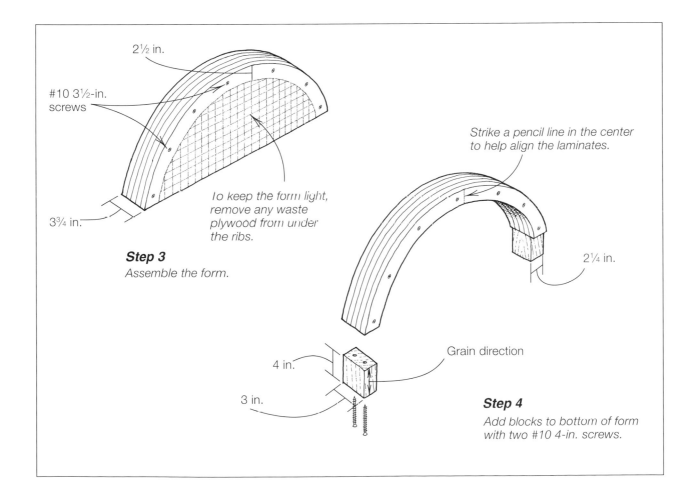

2½ in.

#10 3½-in. screws

3¾ in.

To keep the form light, remove any waste plywood from under the ribs.

Step 3
Assemble the form.

Strike a pencil line in the center to help align the laminates.

2¼ in.

4 in.

3 in.

Grain direction

Step 4
Add blocks to bottom of form with two #10 4-in. screws.

Gluing up the lamination

Once the laminates have been cut and machined, stack them and make a pencil mark at the midpoint of the pile (on both edges and across the top piece) so that you'll be able to align them easily during glue up and to align the pile on the bending form. Before applying glue to the laminates, flex each one, looking for problems with cracking or breaking. If one of the laminates cracks slightly during the dry flex, bury it in the center of the stack (because the edge of this lamination will be covered, it is okay to do this). But if the laminate cracks badly or breaks, it will have to be replaced.

For laminating, I prefer to use two-part urea formaldehyde glue (or a two-part epoxy) because it has a long open time, usually 30 minutes at 70°F—more than white or yellow glues. Its long open time allows me to work at a comfortable pace to glue up the laminations. It also exhibits little or no cold creep when properly cured—an important consideration for a lamination that will remain in tension. (Cold creep is the movement that takes place between pieces of wood joined or laminated with white or yellow glues. It could happen several days or even years after the glue has dried completely. Cold creep results in a crazed finish near the area of movement. It is more common with white or yellow glues because they have flexible gluelines, but it rarely occurs with two-part ureas and epoxies, which have rigid gluelines. On a bent lamination, cold creep can cause spring-back.)

Finally, because it sets by catalytic reaction, not water loss, a two-part glue allows the bent lamination to be removed from the bag as soon as the reaction is complete. (Mix a little extra glue in a plastic container. When it reaches the consistency of hard rubber, you'll know the glue in the bag has set.) The set time varies with shop temperature and the amount of hardener, but the average is three hours at 75°F. Mix a batch, keeping in mind the measurement of 1 oz. per sq. ft. of substrate. Then place the laminates glue side up on the workbench, brush on the glue and begin to assemble the lamination. If you've never used a two-part formaldehyde glue, be sure to experiment with a piece of scrap substrate material because some substrates are more porous and need more glue.

Pressing the lamination

With the glue applied, align the laminates with the center mark on the bending form. Place a sheet of 4-mil poly on the form so that the form won't stick to the lamination. Then put the laminates on the form, aligning the center marks. To keep the pieces aligned until pressure is applied, tightly wrap a strip of packing tape around the center marks (photo below). Stabilizing the ends is trickier. If intimate contact is to be achieved throughout the lamination, the pieces must be allowed some movement. So tie rope loosely around the ends of the laminate and the bottom of the form to hold the sandwich together. (Although they work for thinner laminations, plastic strapping and surgical tubing are not strong enough to hold six oak laminates.)

Place the platen and the form in the bag and turn on the pump. After about three hours, remove the form from the vacuum bag and set aside the workpiece to cure overnight. Then remove excess glue with a cabinet scraper and flush the edges of the lamination with a plane. Then cut the apron to length.

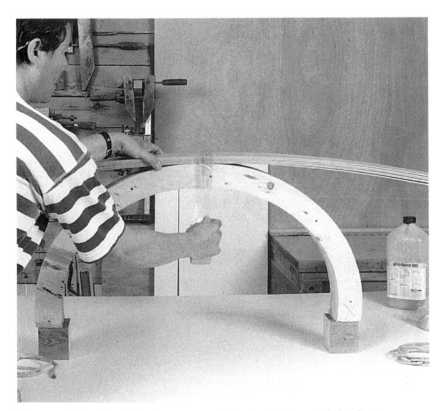

Wrap a strip of packing tape around the laminates and the form to keep them in position until they are placed in the bag.

Cutting and Veneering the Curved Legs

To simplify the layout and cutting of the legs and to ensure uniformity, make ¼-in. Masonite templates of the leg profiles. Trace the profile of each leg on a piece of 8/4 red oak. Then cut each leg and save the waste from the curves, which will be used as cauls later. The kerf marks on the legs will telegraph to the surface of the veneer. To clean up the kerf marks, run the flat sides of the legs lightly through the jointer; on the curves use a cabinet scraper. Scrape the waste pieces to match a leg so that you have a caul to help with the application of veneer (photos below). It's a good idea to spend some time mating the cauls to the legs to ensure that the veneer will be pressed evenly in all areas when it is sandwiched between the cauls.

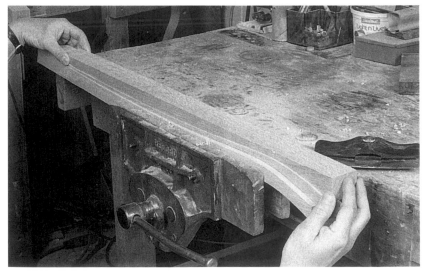

Make cauls for the curved sections of the legs from scrap oak that is left over from cutting. To prepare the cauls, scrape them first (above), then check for fit with the leg (left).

Once the legs have been cut, make a mortise in the flat section, or block, at the top of each leg for the apron. The mortise is cut on the bandsaw. Make the cut slightly narrower than the thickness of the apron (¾ in.), then refine the fit with a gouge. Round the inside surfaces of the joint to conform to the convex and concave curves of the front apron; the final fit should be snug but should not require excessive force to fit the apron. The extra wood at the base of the cut is pared away with a flat chisel until it is 3½ in., or the depth of the finished apron. This joint can also be cut after the leg has been veneered, following the same procedures; be sure to cut carefully, however, to avoid tearing out the veneer.

To veneer the eight flat sides of the legs, cut eight rectangular sheets of veneer and tape them between two pieces of ¼-in. Masonite. Then make a paper template ⅛ in. larger all around than the leg and glue it to the top piece of Masonite with spray adhesive (photo below). Take the whole sandwich to the bandsaw and cut it out. This saves time because all eight pieces of veneer are cut at once.

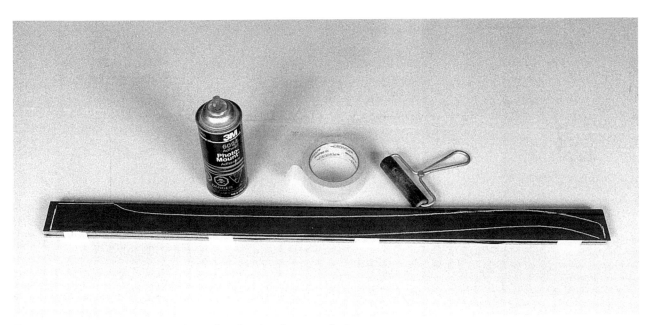

To ensure uniformity of cut, place the sheets of veneer between two pieces of ¼-in. Masonite, then glue a paper template to the top piece of Masonite with spray adhesive. Cut the whole sandwich on the bandsaw.

Cut the veneer for the curved sections of the legs using the same method, but leave a little extra length here because the veneer must conform to the curve of each leg. Cut the sheets for the backs of the legs even longer to allow for the block at the top of the leg. After cutting the sheets for the blocks, number them so that the figure will match the veneer on the rest of the leg, then set the veneer sheets for the blocks aside for now.

The method for gluing the veneer to the flat side of a leg is the same as that described on pp. 80-83. It is possible to veneer two sides of a leg at one time by using the ¼-in. veneer template as a caul, but remember to place a sheet of 4-mil poly between the veneer and the caul (photo below); otherwise, the veneer could stick to the caul.

To veneer the curved sides of the legs, a similar technique is used. Hold the veneer in position with bits of masking tape and then sandwich it between the curved cauls, which are made from the waste oak (see p. 102). Also, be sure to put 4-mil poly between the veneer and the caul. If there is too much veneer overhang, the bag will break it off, which may damage the finish face, so allow only ¹⁄₁₆ in. all around. Then place the leg in the bag and turn on the press. I veneer four legs

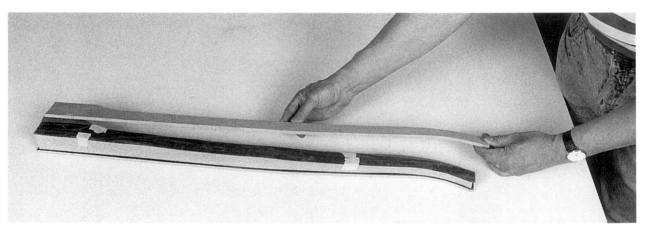

To veneer two sides of a leg at once, use the ¼-in. Masonite template as a caul to press the top piece of veneer. A piece of 4-mil poly between the veneer and the caul keeps the two from sticking together.

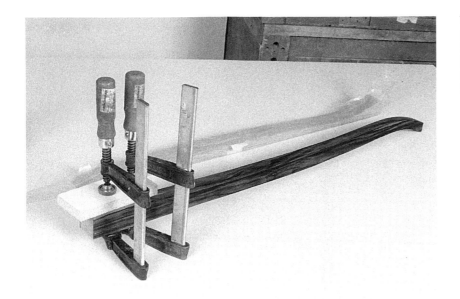

Veneer the back block of each leg with a melamine caul and a hand clamp. The veneer should be cut from the same strip used to cover the curved section of the leg so that the figure will match.

at a time, but when you're starting out, I'd recommend doing one at a time. Because there is limited overhang, the edge can be cleaned up with a cabinet scraper or an abrasive board. The last step is to veneer the block of the back of each leg with clamps and a melamine caul, as shown in the photo above.

Assembling the Table

Once all surfaces are veneered, it's time to put the pieces together. First, attach the legs to the apron, dropping the apron into the mortises and screwing it in from the back. Then add four cleats to the apron, put the tabletop on and drive screws through the cleats and into the top from below. For more information about this table's construction, see the drawing on p. 85. The legs are capped with walrus-tusk ivory feet, but such exotic feet are not necessary. Then the demilune table is ready to be prepared for final finishing. If the piece is to be located on a hardwood floor, protect the floor by putting some simple felt pads on the bottom of the legs.

CHAPTER 7
Advanced Vacuum Veneering

Once the beginning and intermediate techniques of vacuum veneering have been mastered, it is possible to move to the next level, which involves the creation and veneering of curved panels. The vacuum press allows a woodworker to expand from simple, rectilinear design to the unlimited universe of curvilinear form.

In this chapter you'll learn how to construct a form to laminate a panel with multiple curves, and about glues particularly suited to this kind of work. You'll also see a technique for joining straight-grained veneers, as well as a method to prevent tearout on crumbly, highly figured veneers.

As has been done in previous chapters, I'm going to demonstrate techniques discussed by building a specific piece. The example in this chapter is a coffee table with a laminated curved base and top veneered with African satinwood and edged with black walnut. The table is shown on the cover of this book (for construction details, see the drawing on the facing page).

A COFFEE TABLE VENEERED IN THE VACUUM PRESS

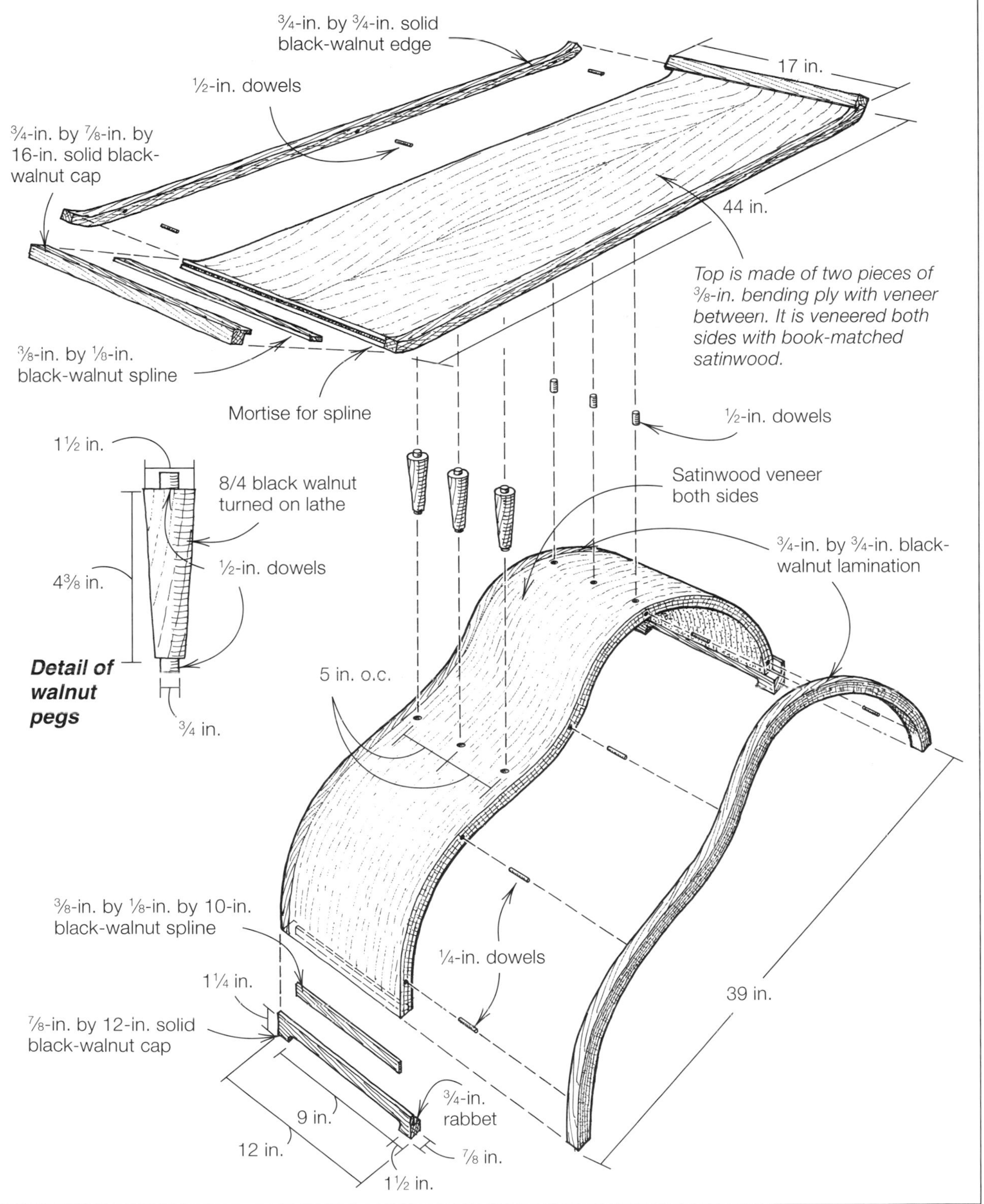

¾-in. by ¾-in. solid black-walnut edge
17 in.
½-in. dowels
¾-in. by ⅞-in. by 16-in. solid black-walnut cap
44 in.
Top is made of two pieces of ⅜-in. bending ply with veneer between. It is veneered both sides with book-matched satinwood.
⅜-in. by ⅛-in. black-walnut spline
Mortise for spline
½-in. dowels
1½ in.
8/4 black walnut turned on lathe
Satinwood veneer both sides
¾-in. by ¾-in. black-walnut lamination
½-in. dowels
4⅜ in.
Detail of walnut pegs
5 in. o.c.
¾ in.
⅜-in. by ⅛-in. by 10-in. black-walnut spline
¼-in. dowels
1¼ in.
39 in.
⅞-in. by 12-in. solid black-walnut cap
¾-in. rabbet
9 in.
12 in.
⅞ in.
1½ in.

This bending form was built to create the laminated curved base for the coffee table shown on the cover.

I don't think it is necessary to construct a bending form tailored to a specific design, especially if it is a first attempt at a vacuum-formed panel. I feel it is more fun to go with the flow and let the curves speak for themselves. The form shown above is the result of an experiment to produce a laminated curved panel for the base of the coffee table. If you prefer, you can purchase forms in a variety of shapes and sizes that lend themselves to vacuum veneering (the manufacturer of your vacuum system can probably help you find a source for prebuilt forms).

Creating a Large Bending Form

I build my large bending forms out of ¾-in. spruce plywood (sheathing grade), bending plywood and 2x scraps. I use the spruce ply for the ribs of a bending form because it is cheaper than fir and stronger than particleboard. However, if the ribs of the form are not higher than 3 in., you can use particleboard, which is less expensive than the spruce ply but less sturdy. But experience has taught me that a collapsed form and ruined workpiece could be the results of skimping on materials for a bending form.

For the skin of a bending form (as well as for the substrate of a curved panel), I recommend using ⅜-in. bending plywood, which solidifies the form and provides an unblemished surface on which to bend the panel. Bending plywood is also marketed as wacky wood or wiggle board. It's is made up of three plies. The grain direction of the inner ply runs perpendicular to the grain of the outer plies, which gives the plywood strength. The grain of the outer plies runs in the same direction, which gives the plywood its bending characteristic (drawing below). Depending on the grain orientation, the sheet can bend in the

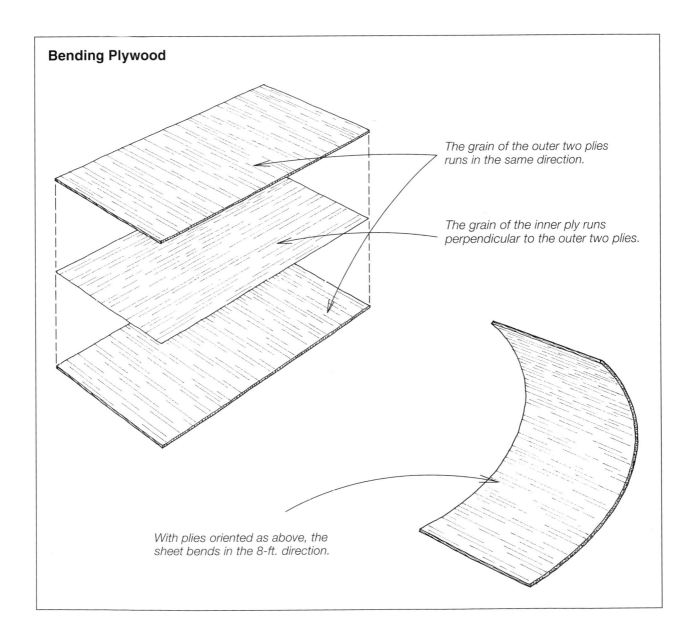

Bending Plywood

The grain of the outer two plies runs in the same direction.

The grain of the inner ply runs perpendicular to the outer two plies.

With plies oriented as above, the sheet bends in the 8-ft. direction.

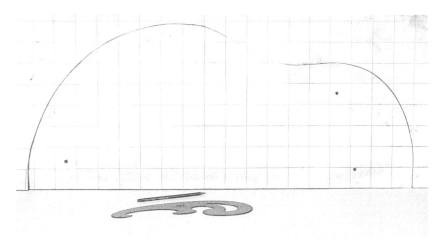

Sketch a rib on paper with a grid of 2-in. squares, refine the form using French curves, then glue the paper to a sheet of Masonite.

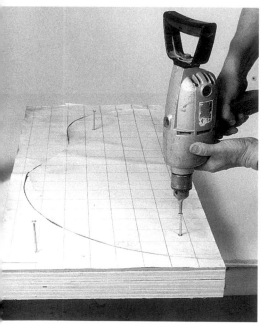

Stack the three ribs, with the template on top, and then screw them together from both sides.

8-ft. direction or the 4-ft. direction. Bending plywood is so flexible that a 4x8 sheet can be rolled and transported in the rear seat of a four-door car. It may be available in your lumberyard, but it's more commonly available from suppliers of cabinetmaking materials.

To make a large bending form for a panel with multiple curves, you first must design a template for the ribs. Make a grid of 2-in. squares on a sheet of white paper (photographic backdrop paper is excellent for this because it comes in long, wide sheets) and attach it to a sheet of ¼-in. Masonite with spray adhesive. Then roughly sketch a rib onto the paper and refine the form with French curves (photo above). When you have achieved a smooth, flowing design, cut the Masonite down on the table saw so that you are left with a rectangular template that contains just the drawing of the rib.

When using plywood ribs in a form, space them 6 in. on center (o.c.); particleboard ribs should be spaced 4 in. o.c. The bending form for the base of the coffee table needs three ribs because the form is 12 in. wide. Cut three pieces of ¾-in. plywood to the same dimensions as the rectangular template, then stack the pieces with the template on top. Align the pile and drive wood screws from both sides to hold the stack together (photo left). Locate the screws away from the cutline and countersink the heads. If the screw tips protrude, file them flush with the plywood (photo facing page) so that they won't catch while you're sawing the template.

File the tips of the screws flush with the plywood so that they do not catch while you're cutting the template on the bandsaw.

Take the whole sandwich to the bandsaw and carefully cut along the template line with a six-tooth $\frac{1}{4}$-in. blade. This blade produces a smooth cut with little need to file high or low points afterward. If you do need to fix high or low spots on the ribs, do so while the pieces are attached. I cut ribs in one pile to ensure a good match—unmatched ribs can produce a skewed form, and worse, a skewed workpiece.

Before taking apart the rib sandwich, drill large holes in the ribs to allow air to escape from inside the form as the vacuum is drawn. Without these holes, the difference in atmospheric pressure between outside the form and inside could cause the structure to explode, similar to how a tightly sealed house could explode during a tornado. The explosion will destroy your form and tear the bag.

The bottom of the form is a 12-in. by 37-in. piece of $\frac{3}{4}$-in. spruce ply cut to size on the table saw. Drill large holes in it to ensure that air evacuates from the form. As the bag envelops the form, it may obstruct holes in the outside ribs, causing the pump to cycle erratically and draw an insufficient vacuum. Air holes drilled in the bottom of the form cannot become plugged in this manner because the kerfs in the platen allow air movement.

Once the air holes are drilled, draw a grid of pencil lines with the help of a straightedge to locate the screws. Then clamp an outside rib upside down, and start driving the #8 $1\frac{3}{4}$-in. screws. (The extra girth of a

Bracing the form keeps the ribs from collapsing inward during pressing. The braces are installed 9 in. o.c. with 1¾-in. screws.

#10 screw can split the plywood laminates.) You won't need to drill pilot holes; the screws can be driven directly into the soft spruce. Attach each rib in this manner.

Under vacuum, the bag will push the outside ribs toward the center of the form, so the ribs must be braced all around with scraps of 2x2 or whatever is handy in the shop (photo above). For this form, the braces are about 5¾ in. long and are screwed from the outside ribs with #8 1¾-in. screws. The size of the braces depends on the width of the form and on the number of ribs. Without proper bracing, the pressure in the bag would collapse the form, ruining the workpiece. I recommend testing the strength of all of your forms under full vacuum before they are put into service.

Now it's time to attach the skin of bending plywood. To find the length of the skin, place a piece of string or rope (use line that will not stretch) along the curve of a rib and mark the rope with a black marker (you can also cut the rope, but remember to tape the ends so that they don't become frayed). Transfer the measurement from the rope to the plywood and cut the sheet to length (58¾ in.). Then rip the panel to 12 in., the width of the form.

Attach the skin to the ribs with #6 1½-in. screws, working from the middle toward either end, flattening the bending ply to the form as you go to ensure a flat, unbuckled form (left photo, below). Countersink the screws and fill the holes with wood putty to maintain a smooth bending surface (right photo, below).

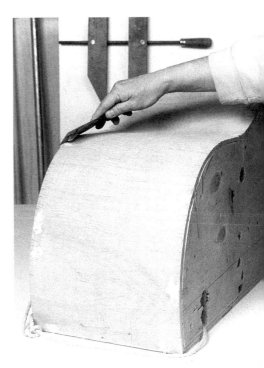

Attach the ⅜-in. skin to the ribs with screws (above). Start in the middle of the form and work toward either end so that you don't create a bump in the skin. Countersink the heads and fill the holes with wood putty (right).

Laminating a Panel
with Multiple Curves

To create the curved base of this coffee table, laminate together two layers of the bending plywood with a layer of backer-grade veneer between for stability. Rip the plies to width the same time you rip the skin of the bending form. The length of each ply must exceed that of the previous one because the circumference of the form increases with each new layer of plywood—in this case by a total of about 1 in. Cut the backer-grade veneer to length with scissors, or a knife and a straightedge. If you are lucky, the veneer will be wide enough to cover the width of the form without a join. When ordering backer-grade veneer, request widths of 12 in. or greater so that you can cut down on the number of joins and, if possible, eliminate them. Doing so will save you some time. The top laminate is 58½ in. long, the backer-grade veneer is 57¾ in. long, and the bottom laminate is 57½ in. long. All pieces are 12 in. wide.

As I mentioned in Chapter 6, for laminating curved panels, I prefer a two-part epoxy or urea glue, both of which are set by a catalyst. Apply the two-part epoxy to the plywood laminates with a trowel and a foam roller, using 1¼ oz. to 1½ oz. per sq. ft. More glue is used here than normal because bending ply is more porous than MDF.

With the glue applied, place the veneer between the two layers of bending ply on the form (top photo, facing page). Position the workpiece on the bending form and secure the concave curve with an elastic cord (available at any hardware store) that hooks into holes drilled in both sides of the form (middle photo, facing page). (Simply expand the air holes drilled when you cut the ribs.) The cord maintains constant pressure at the low point until the bag takes over. Secure the ends of the laminates with loosely tied rope run through the air holes on each end of the ribs (bottom photo, facing page).

For this form, the size of the platen must be reduced to allow the bag sufficient slack to envelop the workpiece. Cut the platen down and check to make sure you have enough slack in the bag using the formula on p. 101. Once you're sure there's enough slack in the bag, place the workpiece in the bag (top photo, p. 116). With the form and the platen in the bag, you should be able to close the bag without a problem (bottom photo, p. 116).

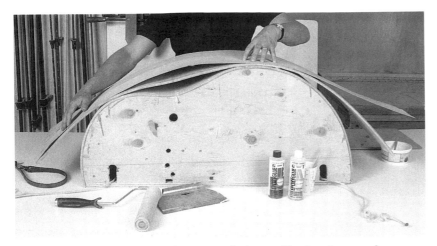

Place a layer of backer-grade veneer between the two layers of bending ply. Apply two-part epoxy to the plywood only, using a trowel and a foam paint roller.

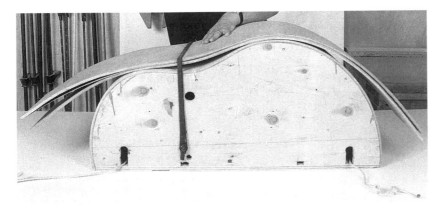

An elastic cord maintains pressure on the bending ply at the concave point of the form until the vacuum takes over.

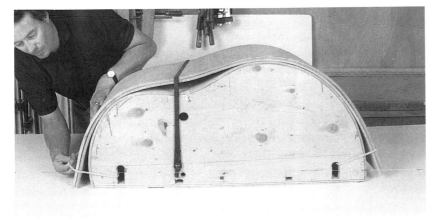

Hold the ends of the laminates close to the form with rope. Tie the rope loosely to allow movement so that a warp or bubble is not created in the panel during pressing.

After cutting the platen down to ensure enough slack in the bag so that it envelops the workpiece, slide the platen and workpiece into the bag.

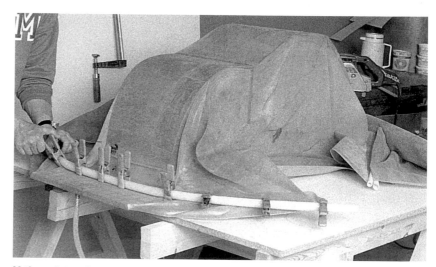

If the platen is of the correct size, you should have no problem sealing the bag.

If you can't close the bag easily, it means that the platen is too big, or the workpiece is too tall. For a curved form of medium height such as this, the platen can simply be cut down. But a very tall form must be placed on its side to fit in the bag. In this case, construct a special platen to allow the bag to envelop the curved section of the workpiece. To make the platen, lay the workpiece and form on a platen. Trace the curves and make another line ½ in. inside the outline of the curves.

This line is the cutline. Make the cut and place the workpiece back on the platen, making sure that it overhangs the platen by about ½ in. so that the bag can completely envelop the form and the laminates.

Pressing the lamination

With the workpiece sealed tightly in the bag, switch on the pump and push the bag into the concave curve of the form with your hand (photo below). This helps the bag conform snugly to the low point and prevents the vinyl from being pinched between the outside ribs and the laminates, especially if the elastic cord lacks strength to hold them tightly to the form. Vacuum bags tend to press convex shapes more readily than concave ones and often require this kind of assistance at the start.

With a large- or medium-sized bending form, it will take several minutes for the pump to reach its full vacuum of 25 Hg (photo p. 118). The pump should maintain the vacuum for at least an hour before recycling. If the pump recycles every five minutes or so, you probably need to patch the bag (for more on patching the bag and maintaining the system, see Chapter 9).

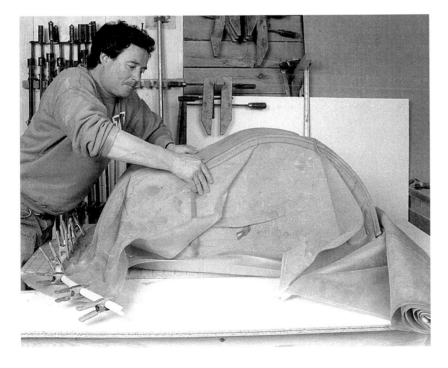

With the pump on, push the bag into the concave curve of the form to help the bag conform to the curve and to keep the bag from being pinched between the laminates and the outside ribs.

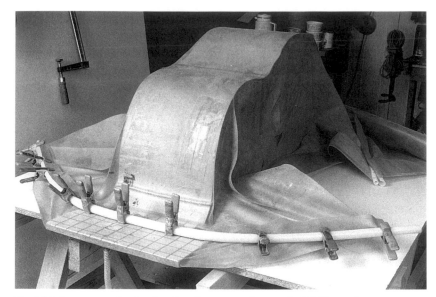

It will take several minutes for the pump to reach 25 Hg and to pull the bag tightly against the form.

A lamination that is glued with epoxy can be removed as soon as the catalytic reaction is complete (about three hours at 75°F, or check the manufacturer's recommendation). If white or yellow glue is used, leave the workpiece under vacuum for at least four hours at 70°F. Once the glue has set, put aside the workpiece to cure overnight before doing any more work on it.

Veneering a Panel with Multiple Curves

Throughout the book I have demonstrated several methods to cut and join veneer. If you were going to apply a backer-grade veneer to the underside of the curved base, I would recommend using a simple cutting method that works well with straight-grained or backer-grade veneers. With this method, sandwich the sheets between two sheets of Masonite (you can use whatever sheet material is available in your shop, as long as the edges are square) and shoot the edges all at once with a plane (photo facing page). Keep the plane flat on the table so that the edge of the veneer is jointed at 90°. Then it's a simple process to join the sheets (for two methods of joining veneer, see pp. 24-26).

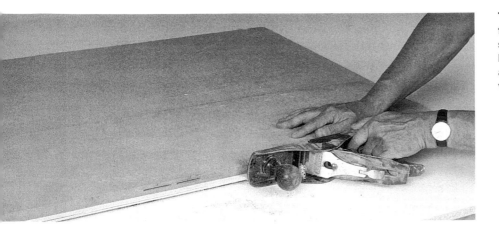

To prepare a good joining edge for straight-grained veneers, sandwich a group of sheets between pieces of Masonite and shoot the edges of the veneer with a plane.

However, the design of this table calls for African satinwood on both sides of the base, so a less-orthodox approach to cutting is needed because satinwood is highly figured and rippled, which make it difficult to cut and join (for a special method of cutting rippled veneers, see the sidebar below).

Once the sheets are joined, you can veneer the curved base similarly to the way the demilune apron was veneered in Chapter 6. Once again, I suggest veneering only one side of the panel at a time until you've gained sufficient experience in the process.

Preparing Rippled or Buckled Veneer for Joining

A rippled or buckled veneer needs to be stabilized before it is finish-cut and joined. Making two-ply veneer is the traditional way of stabilizing veneers. It can be sanded before being glued in position (for more on making two-ply veneers, see p. 76), which eliminates the need to sand or scrape a concave surface, which is time-consuming and aggravating. But creating two-ply veneers for a

long substrate like this base would have been difficult, so here's a different technique that I've used to stabilize the edge of the veneer.

The table's base is 12 in. wide, so for each side you need three sheets of veneer about 4 in. wide and 58½ in. long. Rough-cut each sheet with the veneer saw ½ in. wider than necessary, which leaves ¼-in. waste on both sides for the finish cut. To stabilize the veneer, run a strip of ¾-in. masking tape the length of each edge to be joined (apply the masking tape to the glue side), and with a straightedge

and a utility knife, slice off the waste, leaving about ⅛ in. on each sheet for the overhang.

Even though the tape stabilizes the edge, it is still slightly ragged. So sandwich all of the veneer sheets between two sheets of Masonite and shoot the edges with an abrasive board until a suitable joining surface is achieved. (Don't use a plane here because it will tear out the veneer.) Finally, carefully remove the masking tape from the sheets. That done, join the sheets using either method discussed on pp. 24-26.

Before applying glue, put the base on the bending form, place a sheet of veneer on it and a caul on top of that. Because the caul must bend around curves, use bending plywood. Cut the caul to sufficient length to cover the veneer, but not so long as to prevent the form from sitting flat on the platen. If the caul exceeds the length of the bending form, a gap between the caul and the workpiece could develop during pressing, resulting in an area of veneer that is not firmly attached to the substrate. The caul also should not exceed the width of the veneer or form because the overhang will cause an uneven distribution of pressure, forcing the outside edges down, and the center of the caul up, which will result in poor adhesion in the middle of the workpiece.

After aligning the pieces, draw a chalkline on their edges to help register them easily during glue up (photo below). With the line drawn, remove the caul and the veneer from the base. Now you're ready for glue up.

On a wide panel such as this, apply the glue to the substrate with the trowel and the roller to speed up the procedure. Again, use the two-part epoxy because it has a long open time. With the glue spread, align the veneer with the chalkline on the substrate. Cut a piece of 4-mil poly wide enough so that it covers the edges of the substrate and the veneer. The poly prevents the veneer from sticking to the caul. Hold the veneer and the poly in place with masking tape. Because the tape

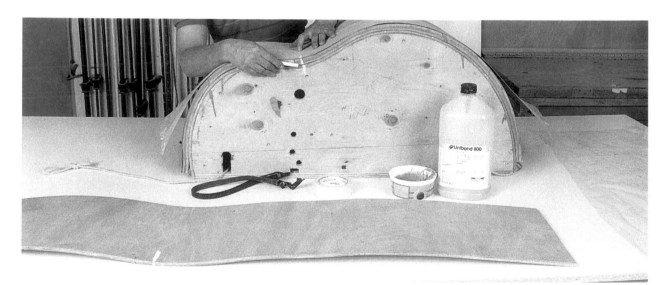

Before glue up, place the lamination on the form, align the veneer and the caul, and mark the pile with a chalkline. The chalkline makes it easy to align the pile after the glue has been applied.

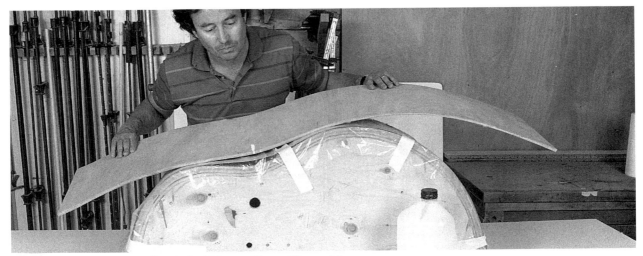

With the veneer and 4-mil poly held in position with masking tape, align the caul with the chalkline.

is applied to the poly only, it does not stick to the veneer when the vacuum is drawn. Place the caul on top of that, align it (photo above) and secure the ends with loosely tied rope.

Then place the workpiece in the bag and turn on the pump. After about three hours, take the workpiece out of the bag and set it aside to cure overnight. Then you're ready to veneer the bottom of the base. It's basically done the same way as the top of the base, but there are a few differences.

Here the bending form will serve as the caul. Spread two-part epoxy on the bottom of the curved base and attach the veneer to the base with bits of masking tape to keep it in registration. Then place a sheet of 4-mil poly on the bending form, place the base on the form, roll it into the bag and turn on the pump. After about three hours, remove the workpiece from the bag, pull the base off the bending form, and let it cure overnight.

Making and Veneering the Curved Tabletop

The top of the coffee table is formed with the same techniques used to create the curved base. First, build a 2¾-in. high curved form made of ¾-in. spruce plywood, as shown in the drawing on p. 122. Because of the great pressure exerted upon the workpiece in the bag, you'll need

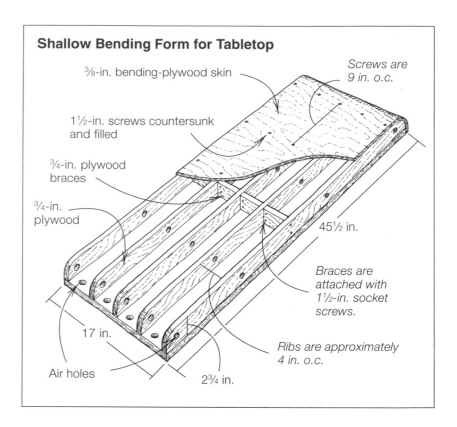

Shallow Bending Form for Tabletop

⅜-in. bending-plywood skin

Screws are 9 in. o.c.

1½-in. screws countersunk and filled

¾-in. plywood braces

¾-in. plywood

45½ in.

Braces are attached with 1½-in. socket screws.

17 in.

Ribs are approximately 4 in. o.c.

Air holes

2¾ in.

to brace the form in the middle. A longer form will require more braces. However, a braced form can still be damaged under vacuum; this is especially true when a composition material like particleboard is used. (Inflatable bladders—a new technology in veneering—support a form as well as braces do and simplify form building. For more on inflatable bladders, see the sidebar on the facing page.)

The top is a bent lamination consisting of a sheet of 17-in. wide by 44-in. long backer-grade veneer sandwiched between two pieces of ⅜-in. bending ply cut to the same dimensions (for the technique, see p. 114). Place the sandwich on the bending form, with rope loosely tied around the ends. Place the workpiece on its platen in the bag, seal the bag and turn on the pump. After about three hours, pull the workpiece out of the bag and let the top cure overnight. Then trim the top down to its finished dimensions.

The satinwood veneer on both sides of the tabletop is book-matched, using the techniques I discussed earlier in this chapter. After trimming the veneer, install edges on both the base and the top.

Inflatable Bladders Simplify Form Construction

The top of the coffee table used as the example in this chapter was formed on a 2¾-in. high, well-braced plywood form. The use of an inflatable bladder would have simplified the form's construction by eliminating most of the ribs and all of the bracing, without any loss of strength. Inflatable bladders are made of rugged 15-mil clear

polyurethane. They have reinforced seams and can be connected together to fill large spaces or separate compartments in cabinets. Bladders are available in six sizes, ranging from 2x3 to 4x10, and the kits usually come with all the necessary fittings and hoses. (For more information, contact the companies listed on p. 67.)

To build a form with an inflatable bladder, you would need just two ribs and the base (see drawing below). You would also need to attach another nipple to the bag.

Place the form in the bag on its platen and inflate the bladder until the bending-plywood skin begins to bulge. Then disconnect the tube from the exhaust port of the pump to the extra nipple on the bag and turn on the vacuum pump. The nipple on the bag that connects to the bladder is left open, equalizing pressure between outside the bag and inside the form, thus keeping the form stable against the forces of the vacuum.

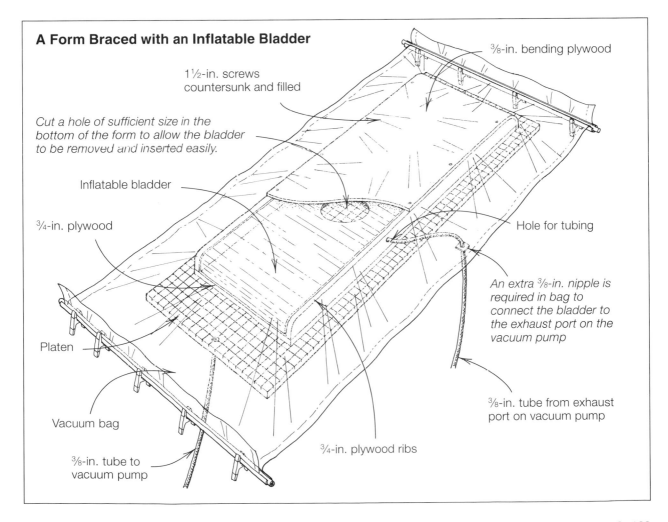

A Form Braced with an Inflatable Bladder

⅜-in. bending plywood

1½-in. screws countersunk and filled

Cut a hole of sufficient size in the bottom of the form to allow the bladder to be removed and inserted easily.

Inflatable bladder

¾-in. plywood

Hole for tubing

An extra ⅜-in. nipple is required in bag to connect the bladder to the exhaust port on the vacuum pump

Platen

⅜-in. tube from exhaust port on vacuum pump

Vacuum bag

¾-in. plywood ribs

⅜-in. tube to vacuum pump

Laminating Curved Edges
for the Base of the Table

Each side of the coffee-table base is edged with a ¾-in. thick bent lamination of black walnut, and each end is capped with solid black walnut (for installation details, see the drawing on p. 107). To make the bent laminations, use the same form you used to bend the base.

To make each of the base's curved edges, first rip a piece of 8/4 black walnut 2 in. wide by 64 in. long. Then rip the piece into six laminates about ³⁄₁₆ in. thick and plane each laminate to a thickness of ¹³⁄₁₆ in. (planing also cleans up the saw kerfs).

The stack of laminates must be shorter than the circumference of the bending form (58¾ in.) so that it won't interfere with the platen, so trim it to 58 in. Then dry-bend the stack around the form to make sure the laminates will make the bend without cracking or breaking. Press the lamination using the same techniques discussed on pp. 114-118.

The sides of the top were edged with solid black walnut because the curves are not severe. The edges are cut on the bandsaw from 4/4 stock, leaving a little extra on all sides to allow for trimming. The black-walnut caps on the base and the top are all cut on the bandsaw from 4/4 stock. The caps are rabbeted on one side to overlap the top.

Assembling the Coffee Table

The black-walnut edges are attached to the top and the base with ¼-in. dowels and glue. You have the option of using the vacuum press (photo facing page) or traditional methods to attach the edges. After attaching the edges, flush them to the surface with a cabinet scraper. The caps for the top and the base are rabbeted and splined and attached with glue.

The tabletop is attached to the high point of the convex curve of the base with glue and ½-in. dowels. It is attached to the low point of the curve with turned black-walnut pegs, glue and dowels. Once the table is assembled, let it sit overnight to cure, and then it's ready to be finished.

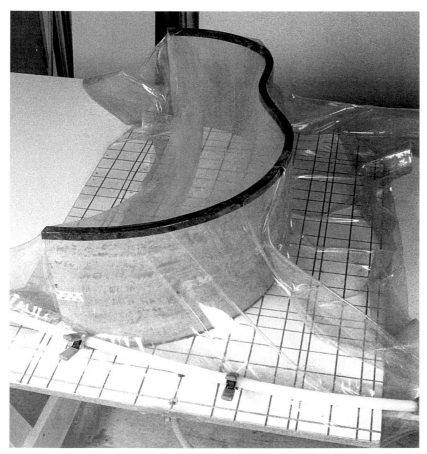

The edges of the base of the table are capped with bent laminations of black walnut and are glued to the panel in the vacuum bag using dowels for registration.

CHAPTER 8

Other Uses for the Vacuum Press

To this point, I have demonstrated some of the most obvious uses for a vacuum press: veneering and laminating pieces. These are techniques I employ daily in my shop to construct furniture. But this versatile tool can perform other jobs—not necessarily veneering related—and in this chapter, I present some of the most helpful and practical uses for a small shop.

The Vacuum Press as a Clamping System

Gluing up boards to create a wide panel used to be a tedious, messy job that involved a number of bar clamps. Not any more. The versatile vacuum press can make the task cleaner and less stressful. But to be effective, the system requires you to be a bit more fussy in preparing the boards for glue up.

First, cut a platen that's ½ in. smaller in width than the workpiece and a bit longer (drawing facing page). Carefully plane away a small amount of wood from the contact edge of each board in the center (drawing facing page). The result will be a board that is a hair narrow-

Gluing up Boards in the Vacuum Press

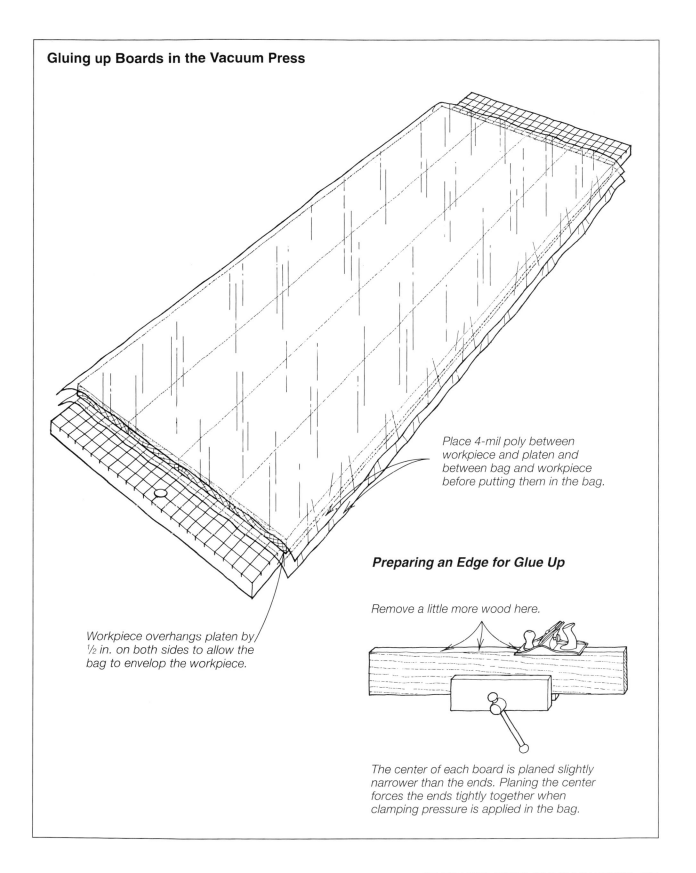

Place 4-mil poly between workpiece and platen and between bag and workpiece before putting them in the bag.

Workpiece overhangs platen by ½ in. on both sides to allow the bag to envelop the workpiece.

Preparing an Edge for Glue Up

Remove a little more wood here.

The center of each board is planed slightly narrower than the ends. Planing the center forces the ends tightly together when clamping pressure is applied in the bag.

er in the middle than at the ends. Removing a bit of wood from the center of each board will force the ends tightly together when pressure is applied in the bag.

Place a sheet of 4-mil poly on the platen to prevent glue from seeping onto the platen, then assemble the piece directly on the platen. Test the workpiece under full vacuum before applying glue to the joints, which will give you a good visual indication to the quality of the fit between joints. When you're sure that the joints fit well, apply yellow glue to the contact edge of each board and rub the joints together one at a time until the entire workpiece is assembled. Place a sheet of poly over the workpiece to prevent glue from oozing onto the bag, put it into the bag and switch on the pump. As the panel is pressed, watch carefully to be sure the glue squeezes out evenly along each joint.

With bar clamps, it is easy to apply too much pressure to make up for inconsistencies in the joints. But a bad joint will come apart eventually no matter how much pressure is applied during glue up. With the vacuum press, the joints must be carefully constructed beforehand because the pressure cannot be increased beyond a certain point, although it is more than sufficient to do the job. For this reason, the result can be a panel with superior joints.

Inlaying in a Vacuum

The vacuum press is particularly useful for inlaying a design in a panel, especially on a large panel, where hand clamps may not be able to reach the middle. Also, the vacuum press allows you to use white and yellow glues, which have long open times. Another reason I prefer to use the vacuum press for inlaying instead of hammer or mechanical methods is that it applies pressure evenly to all parts of an inlay. The even distribution of pressure guarantees that the inlay will seat properly and adhere firmly to all areas of the mortise. With the vacuum press, you can easily inlay a panel in a number of locations at one time, a feat that is difficult to accomplish using traditional methods.

Here's how to put an inlay in the center of a panel using the vacuum press. Once you've got your design for the inlay on paper, sandwich a sheet of veneer between two pieces of ¼-in. Masonite (this is the same technique used to cut multiple sheets of veneer for the curved table legs in Chapter 6). Glue your design to the top of the sandwich with spray adhesive and cut the outline on a bandsaw fitted with a fine-tooth blade. I find this the quickest and easiest way to cut out a simple design from a sheet of veneer or multiple sheets of veneer. However, it is also acceptable to use a knife for this job, and you may find this method preferable.

Position the design on the panel and lightly trace the outline onto the panel with a sharp pencil. Then go over the outline with a utility knife. Clear away the veneer in the middle of the outline freehand with a $\frac{3}{8}$-in. straight bit in the router. Cut to within $\frac{1}{32}$ in. of the incision around the inlay. Then clean it up with a palm chisel and check for fit. (For more details about the cutting technique, see pp. 28 and 30.)

Once the inlay fits snugly into its mortise, brush yellow or white glue into the mortise and put the inlay in place. Align the inlay in the mortise and hold it down with masking tape (photo below) because the glue could cause the veneer to curl and lift out of the mortise. Cut a melamine caul of sufficient size to cover all areas of the inlay and place it over the inlay. Then put the workpiece in the vacuum bag and turn on the pump.

Once the glue sets (about an hour for a small workpiece), remove the workpiece from the bag and let it cure overnight before working it further. Then scrape off the masking tape after soaking it with paint thinner (wear rubber gloves and a respirator while working with thinner).

Hold the inlay in position with masking tape because the glue may cause the veneer to curl and lift out of the mortise.

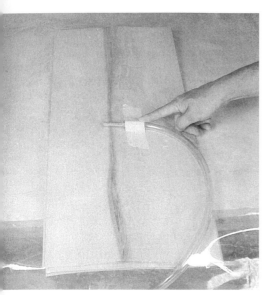

When bending without a platen, run a length of ⅜-in. I.D. vinyl tubing from the faucet tube in the nipple and tape it to the workpiece. This will prevent the exhaust tube from becoming plugged by the bag as the vacuum is drawn.

Bending a Panel Without a Form

The vacuum press can be used to create a small, curved panel without a complicated bending form. This is a technique borrowed from the boat-building industry, and it's not for beginners. It's a lot of fun and can yield some interesting results.

For this type of laminating, I recommend a two-part epoxy with a hardener, although a two-part urea glue can be substituted (just remember that you'll need a glue with a long working time). The lamination can consist of layers of ⅟₁₆-in. birch ply, thin wood laminates or multiple sheets of veneer; choose whatever material will result in a panel of sufficient thickness to hold its shape and meet your design requirements. When using this technique, I follow a plan, but I have never bent a panel according to a specific measurement. To find out how it can be done and for more information on bending without a form, refer to *Advanced Vacuum Bagging Techniques* in the Further Reading section (see p. 159).

For this example, I am going to illustrate how to laminate a curved panel from sheets of backer-grade maple veneer. Glue up the sheets and place them inside the vacuum bag with the platen removed and without a caul, and place 4-mil poly on the workpiece (be sure that the poly will not plug the exhaust tube). With the platen removed from the bag, the ⅜-in. O.D. faucet tube, which fits through the nipple to connect the pump tube to the hole in the platen, protrudes inside the bag by ⅝ in. and could become plugged by the bag under vacuum.

Use an elastic cord to hold the laminates in position until the epoxy sets.

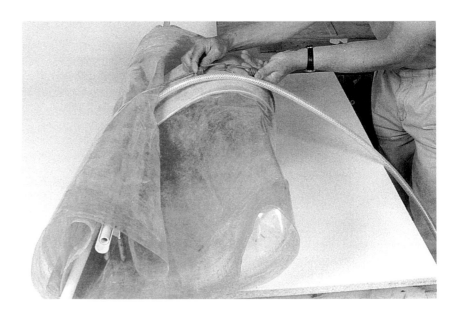

To prevent this, run a suitable length of ⅜-in. I.D. vinyl tubing from the faucet tube in the nipple and tape it to the workpiece. This will keep the pump cycling regularly (left photo, facing page).

Without the platen or the caul, you can manipulate the laminates and the bag into a curved shape while the vacuum is drawn. Sometimes it is necessary to release the vacuum and repeat this process until you achieve the desired results. Once you've got the shape you want, let the pump draw a vacuum of 25 Hg, which, in most cases, will hold the laminates in position. Tie a rope or elastic cord around the bag and the panel until the glue has completely set (bottom photo, facing page).

Veneering Concave and Convex Substrates

The vacuum bag will not conform to intricate shapes, but it can be used to apply veneer to round pieces, such as moldings. To veneer a concave substrate, first support the substrate on cradles cut from

Supporting a Concave Substrate in the Vacuum Bag

¾-in. substrate

Round corners of cradles to protect bag from puncturing.

Cradles cut from scrap 2x6 support the substrate. The cradles are space 4 in. o.c. and are temporarily attached to the substrate.

CHAPTER 9

Vacuum-Press Maintenance

To prolong the life of your vacuum press and to keep it running without trouble, you'll have to keep it in top working order. In this chapter, I'll talk about basic maintenance techniques. Troubleshooting the system is a major part of vacuum-press maintenance. Many of the problems you will experience with the system are easily fixed. The drawing on the facing page gives you some direction on where to search for common problems, both with the bag and with the pump. If you check all the trouble spots shown in the drawing, and you're still having problems with your system, consult with the manufacturer of your press.

Maintaining the Bag

The bag is the least rugged component of the system and will require the most attention and maintenance. But even a homemade 20-mil vinyl bag can last several years if it is treated with care. Over time, you will encounter a few problems, such as holes in the bag and tears in the seams. Here are a few simple solutions to those problems.

Troubleshooting the Vacuum Press

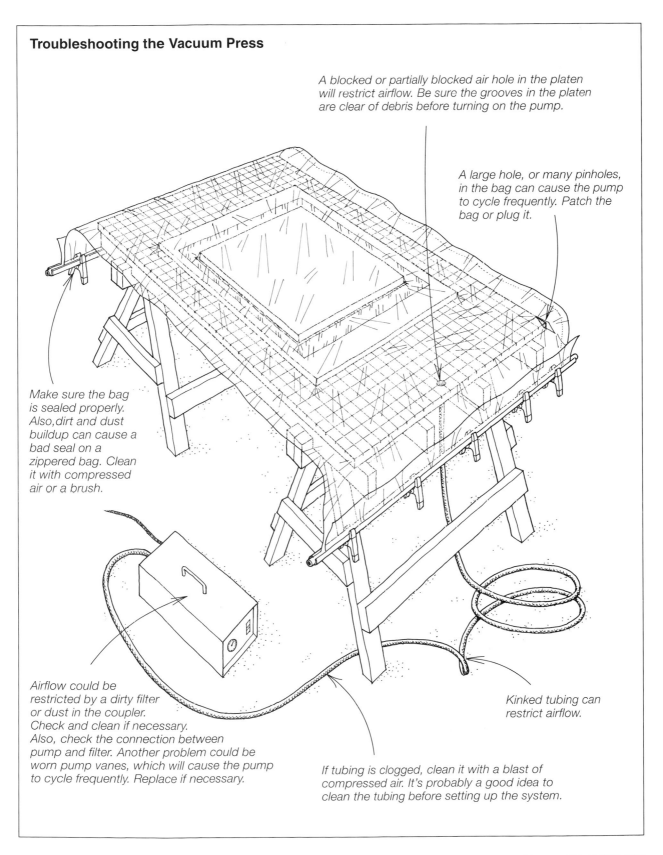

A blocked or partially blocked air hole in the platen will restrict airflow. Be sure the grooves in the platen are clear of debris before turning on the pump.

A large hole, or many pinholes, in the bag can cause the pump to cycle frequently. Patch the bag or plug it.

Make sure the bag is sealed properly. Also, dirt and dust buildup can cause a bad seal on a zippered bag. Clean it with compressed air or a brush.

Airflow could be restricted by a dirty filter or dust in the coupler. Check and clean if necessary. Also, check the connection between pump and filter. Another problem could be worn pump vanes, which will cause the pump to cycle frequently. Replace if necessary.

Kinked tubing can restrict airflow.

If tubing is clogged, clean it with a blast of compressed air. It's probably a good idea to clean the tubing before setting up the system.

Finding and plugging pinholes

If your automatic vacuum press is recycling every five minutes (called short-cycling), or more frequently than usual, there might be a small hole in the bag. Although it will not harm the pump to short-cycle, the noise can be distracting and—if you're the nervous type like myself— make you jump each time the pump cuts in. If there's not an obvious hole in the bag (it could be a pinhole), you should be sure that another, simpler problem isn't making the pump short-cycle: check the bag's seal, make sure the hose connections are tight and look for dust buildup in the coupler (see drawing p. 135). Once you've narrowed the trouble down to a hole—small or large—it's a good idea to patch it before the hole gets bigger.

To locate a pinhole, vacuum-press manufacturers recommend that a diluted mixture of food dye and water be brushed over the outside of the bag while it's under full vacuum. The solution will be sucked through the pinhole, and a small stain will appear on the platen to reveal the location of the leak (photos below). With clear vinyl bags, this technique works well, although it gets a bit messy if the dye is brushed over a very large area.

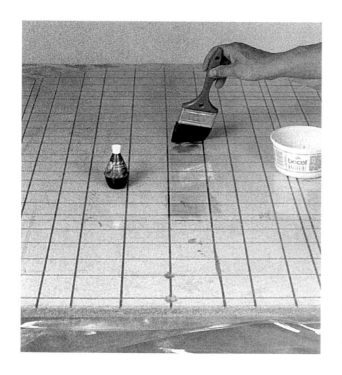

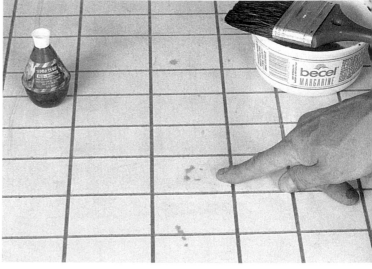

To locate a pinhole, brush a diluted solution of food coloring and water onto the bag while under vacuum (left). Wipe away the solution, and you'll see a stain on the platen at the location of the leak (above).

The first time I had a bag tear during pressing, I was totally unprepared and had to pull the workpiece out of the bag and rebuild it after I patched the bag. Under normal use, about 90% of all leaks can be repaired while the workpiece is under vacuum.

If a small leak develops, seal it with clear packing tape. This is usually sufficient to plug the hole until a permanent repair can be made (top photo, below). For a large tear, cut a patch from a roll of matching vinyl, place it over the hole and seal the edges with clear packing tape (bottom photo, below).

For the woodworker who does a lot of curved pressings, like myself, a backup bag is a good idea. This way, if the bag develops a leak that is inaccessible or too large to fix easily, you can remove the workpiece from the bag and quickly push it into the standby.

For the hobbyist, one bag should be sufficient. However, you can create a simple backup by gluing an extra ⅜-in. nipple on the opposite end of your bag. If your bag tears during pressing, simply turn off the pump and quickly slide the workpiece to the other side of the bag (assuming the workpiece is small enough for this technique to work). Then reseal the bag and turn on the pump. Fortunately, a large tear happens very infrequently during pressing, if you've set up the system carefully.

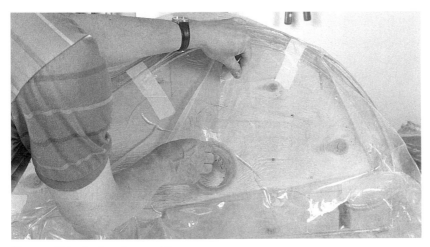

If a small leak develops while work is being pressed, place a piece of clear packing tape over the hole.

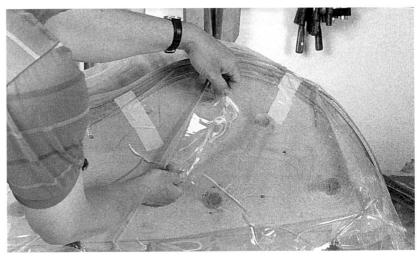

If a large tear occurs while pressing, cut a patch, place it over the hole and seal around the edges with packing tape.

This homemade stethoscope can help locate a pinhole. Hold the flared end on the bag and move the tube slowly across the surface until you can hear an amplified hiss from the leak.

I restrict the search area by finding the general location of the pinhole with a homemade stethoscope while the bag is under full vacuum (photo above). Hold the flared end of a flexible plastic tube against the bag and move the tube slowly across the bag's surface while listening at the other end for the hiss of the leak. Once you hear it, brush a little dye around the area to get a fix on the pinhole. (This is one of those crazy tricks that only a woodworker who has spent too much time alone could devise. The tube I use is actually a child's toy and sells for a few dollars. Any large-diameter, flexible tubing will work just as well.)

Once you've found the pinhole (or holes), wipe the dye from the outside of the bag clean. To plug a pinhole, scuff the vinyl with 220-grit wet/dry paper and acetone, then apply a drop of PVC cement to the hole. It takes about five minutes for the plug to dry. Industrial-quality polyurethane bags can be similarly plugged. They are not as prone to pinholes, however, and require less overall maintenance because of their seamless construction and rugged material.

Patching large holes

A large hole in the bag is often caused by a protruding sharp edge on a workpiece that has not been rounded or covered with protective material. That's why it's a good idea to round the edges of the cauls and the platens you use. Because it may not be possible to remove a sharp edge from a workpiece, place a piece of 20-mil vinyl over the sharp edge or corner to protect the bag from a puncture (photo below). This will also prevent the formation of small raised areas that can disfigure the bag and become the source of future pinholes.

Once I was in a hurry to finish a piece of furniture for a client. In my haste, I inadvertently placed a sheet of veneer on top of the 20-mil bag I had just purchased and began to cut it with a veneer saw. After I had made a long incision in the veneer, I realized my mistake, and with a bad feeling in the pit of my stomach, stopped to examine the damage: a 12-in. slice in the middle of my new bag.

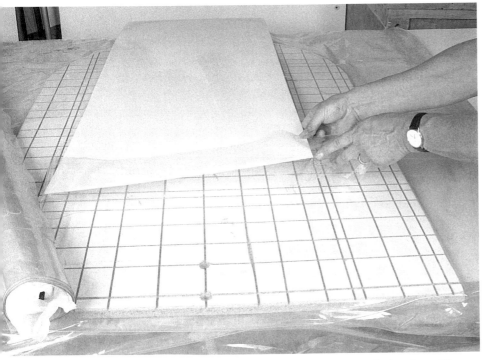

Cover sharp edges with vinyl to protect the bag from being torn. The vinyl will also prevent the formation of small raised areas that can weaken the bag and be a future source of leaks.

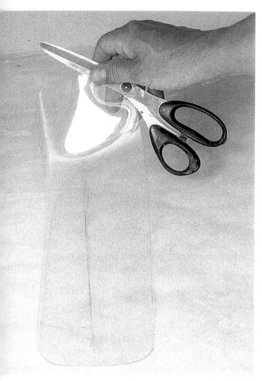

Cut a patch that generously covers the incision.

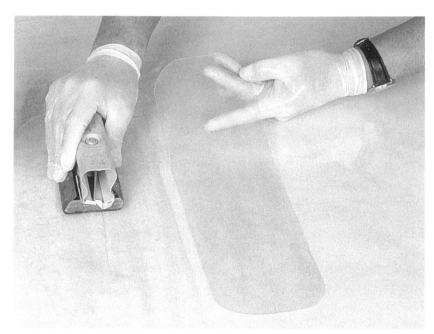

Round the corners of the patch and scuff the glue side with acetone and wet/dry paper. The area around the incision should also be scuffed.

I keep a 54-in. wide roll of 20-mil vinyl in the shop to patch large holes. The patch should match the bag material: e.g., a 30-mil bag should be patched with 30-mil vinyl. In general, make your patches 2 in. larger all around than the hole. To repair a 12-in. hole, prepare a 4-in. by 14-in. patch that generously covers the incision (left photo, above).

Round the corners of the patch and scuff the glue side with acetone and 220-grit wet/dry paper (right photo, above). (Remember to work in a well-ventilated area when working with acetone and wear rubber gloves.) The area around the hole should be prepared the same way. Scuffing clouds the vinyl a little but not enough to make it opaque. (I like to be able to see through the bag so that I can keep an eye on the piece being pressed, checking for registration, etc.) Apply some clear PVC adhesive, which is usually supplied with the bag, to the patch and to the bag. Even though I use spray adhesive at the seams, don't use it to repair holes in a bag. It has a yellow pigment that is opaque and after a few repairs, it could become difficult to see through the bag. Place a sheet of melamine inside the bag, under the patch, and another outside the bag, clamp the sandwich and let it set overnight (photo facing page). If patched correctly, the bag should be able to withstand many more pressings of both flat and curved work.

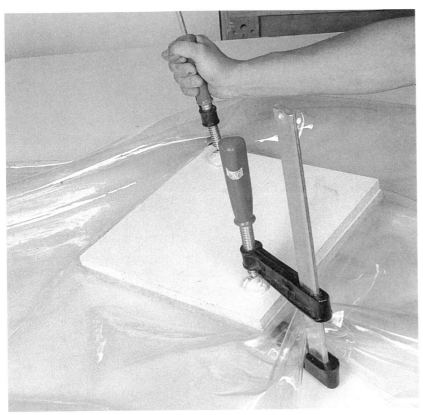

Once the PVC adhesive has been applied, clamp the patch between sheets of melamine overnight.

Repairing and reinforcing seams

The most vulnerable part of a vacuum bag is the seam. Manufactured vinyl bags are heat-sealed to give a strong seam. My 30-mil bag has withstood the demands of many pressings, even curved work; but even it has had its share or tears along the seam. Polyurethane bags, which are manufactured as seamless tubes, are very strong. But these bags are expensive and are designed for a shop that will be doing a lot of production work. (These bags also require a special adhesive to patch holes, which may not be readily available.)

The steps for patching the seam of a bag are the same steps described on the facing page. Scuff the glue side of the patch and round its corners. Then scuff the area around the hole in the seam. Apply clear PVC adhesive to the seam and to the patch, place the patch over the seam, clamp cauls under and above the patch and let it set overnight.

A homemade bag, such as my 20-mil one, works fine for flat pressings, but curved work will really stress the bag's seams. Seams can be reinforced with closer strips of CPVC pipe (see p. 59 for details on how to make the closer strips). Simply place the closer strips on the seams of the bag and clamp them tightly. Also, reducing the platen size by the maximum amount allowable reduces stress on the seams (see p. 101). This is important even with a manufactured vinyl bag.

How to clean and store the bag

After each pressing, use a damp cloth to remove any wet glue that has adhered to the bag. If the glue has already dried, you can simply peel it off the vinyl with your finger (photo left). But you won't be able to do this with a two-part epoxy; it will permanently bond to the vinyl if allowed to dry. That's why I recommend placing 4-mil poly between the workpiece and the interior of the bag. Melamine cauls and platens must similarly be protected because epoxy is a high-saturation glue that tends to bleed excessively through open-grained veneers and, unlike other glues, will stick to melamine. Uncured epoxy can be removed with acetone or denatured alcohol (photo below).

To store a bag, roll it carefully and place it in a clean, dry area, away from sunlight. If the bag has a zipper, dust and wood particles should be removed from it with a toothbrush or compressed air.

Dried glue that has adhered to the bag can be removed by peeling it off the vinyl. If the glue has not set, warm water will remove most of it.

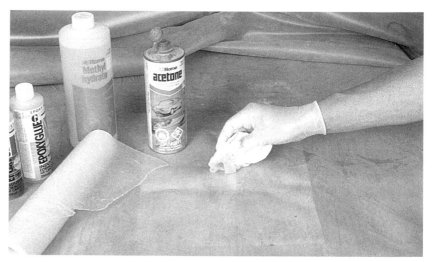

Two-part epoxy will bond permanently to vinyl and melamine if it cures. Uncured epoxy can be removed from the bag with acetone or denatured alcohol.

Pump Maintenance

As I mentioned in Chapter 4, my vacuum system has an oilless 5-cfm rotary-vane pump. I recommend this type of pump for small-shop vacuum pressing because it moves air efficiently, and it requires less maintenance than a piston pump.

Maintenance of the rotary-vane pump is easy. After each pressing, remove the air-filter bowl and clean the element with a brush or compressed air (left photo, below). This is the single most important way to keep the system running at peak efficiency. If done religiously, it will add years to the life of all the components and give trouble-free pressing each time a vacuum is drawn.

It's also important to detach the air hose from the bag at the end of each day and run the pump for about 90 seconds (right photo, below). This draws clean, dry air into the pump and exhausts moist air from the vane chamber that could cause a vane to corrode and lock.

After a few years of service, it is a good idea to check the vanes for wear and, if necessary, replace them (replacement vanes and other parts can be purchased from the manufacturer of your pump). Vanes in most new rotary pumps are made of a carbon compound that allows the vanes to self-adjust as they become worn so that the pump will always perform at top efficiency. If you're having trouble with your pump, or if you need parts, the best option is to call the manufacturer of your system.

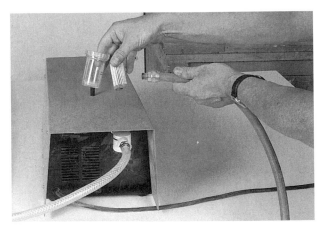

After each pressing, remove the air-filter bowl and clean the element with a brush or compressed air.

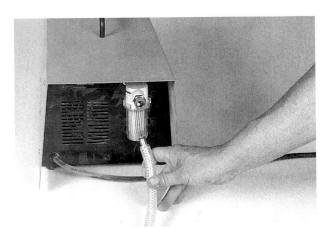

At the end of each day, detach the air hose from the pump and allow clean, dry air to be drawn into the vane chamber for about 90 seconds.

A GALLERY OF VENEERED FURNITURE

Computer cabinet veneered
in maple burl and Australian
lacewood, with birch solids.
Elm and maple inlays
decorate the pilasters.
Photos by Marcus Pearson,
Lomar Productions.

*Designers: Peter Hains and
Mole White Associates.*

*Maker: Peter Hains,
Ontario, Canada.*

Living-room table veneered in blistered big-leaf maple, ebony, ebonized cherry and purpleheart. Photos by Michael C. Fortune

Maker: Michael C. Fortune, Toronto, Canada.

Sideboard veneered in cherry and satinwood, with forged bronze handles and top. Photo by Lee Fatheree.

Maker: Colin Reid, Oakland, Calif.

Demilune table veneered in Macassar ebony. Photo by David Shath Square.

Maker: David Shath Square, Manitoba, Canada.

China cabinet veneered inside with satinwood. Outside is carved solid cherry. Base is wenge veneer. Cabinet features forged bronze handles. Photos by Dick Belcher.

Maker: Colin Reid, Oakland, Calif.

Residential office veneered in bird's-eye maple. Photo by Derik Murray.

Designer: Robert M. Ledingham, Inc.

Maker: Lipton & Son Cabinetmakers, Ltd., British Columbia, Canada.

Coffee table veneered in bubinga, east Indian rosewood, with maple inlay. Legs are capped with solid maple. Photo by Dennis Griggs.

Maker: Darryl Keil, Brunswick, Maine.

Bedroom set veneered in lacewood and Macassar ebony. Photo by Ric Murray.

Maker: Steve Turino, Wakefield, R.I.

Chairs veneered in bird's-eye maple, lacewood and Macassar ebony. Photo by Dean Powell.

Maker: Steve Turino, Wakefield, R.I.

Gift of James Renwick Alliance, museum purchase made possible by the Smithsonian Collections Acquisition Program.

**Cylinder front desk veneered
in Australian lacewood.
Photos by Dean Powell.**

*Maker: Jere Osgood,
Wilton, N.H.*

154

Clock tower veneered in madrone burl and natural and ebonized Swiss pear. Photo by Wayne Dombkowski.

Maker: Jack Alberti, Poquonock, Conn.

At right: Armoire veneered in rift-cut purpleheart and curly english maple. Photo by Naomi Stevens.

Maker: Lipton & Son Cabinetmakers, Ltd., British Columbia, Canada.

Guitar cabinet veneered in satinwood, curly cherry, Macassar ebony and bird's-eye maple. Photos by David Shath Square.

Maker: David Shath Square, Manitoba, Canada.

Cabinet veneered in bee's-wing mahogany, with padauk trim and accents. Photo by Cook Neilson.

Maker: Steve Holman, Dorset, Vt.

FURTHER READING

Books

Advanced Vacuum Bagging Techniques. Gougeon Brothers, Bay City, Mich., 1991 (catalog No. 002-150).

Conservation by Design edited by Scott Landis. The Woodworkers Alliance for Rainforest Protection, Easthampton, Mass., and Museum of Art, Rhode Island School of Design, Providence, R.I., 1993.

The Encyclopedia of Wood: A Tree-by-Tree Guide to the World's Most Valuable Resource by Bill Lincoln et al. Facts on File, Oxford, England, 1989.

Fine Hardwoods Selectorama. The Fine Hardwood Veneer Association and the American Walnut Manufactures Association, Indianapolis, Ind., 1990.

Marquetry by Pierre Ramond. The Taunton Press, Newtown, Conn., 1989.

Marquetry and Inlay: Twenty Decorative Projects by Alan and Gill Bridgewater. Tab Books, Blue Ridge Summit, Pa., 1991.

Masterpieces of Furniture in Photographs and Measured Drawings by Verna C. Salomonsky. Dover Publications, New York, N.Y., 1953.

Modern Woodworking by Willis H. Wagner. The Goodheart Wilcox Co., Inc., South Holland, Ill., 1991.

Ruhlmann: Master of Art Deco by Florence Camard; translated by David Macey. Harry N. Abrams, New York, N.Y., 1993.

Understanding Wood by R. Bruce Hoadley. The Taunton Press, Newtown, Conn., 1981.

The Wright Style: Re-Creating the Spirit of Frank Lloyd Wright by Carl Lind. Simon & Schuster, New York, N.Y., 1992.

Magazine Articles

"Aniline Dyes" by Bob Flexner. *Woodwork,* August 1994; pp. 64-69.

"The Basics of Vacuum Bag Veneering" by David Shath Squarc. *Fine Woodworking,* November 1994; pp. 62-66.

"How Veneer is Made" by David and Abram Loft. *Woodwork,* November 1992; pp. 44-51.

Understory: The Journal of the Woodworkers Alliance for Rainforest Protection. WARP, 289 College St., Burlington, Vt. 05401 (802-862-4448).

"Using Shop-Sawn Veneer" by Paul Harrell. *Fine Woodworking,* August 1994; pp. 44-49.

"Vacuum Veneering" by Greg Elder. *Fine Woodworking,* February 1986; pp. 70-71.

"Vacuum-Bag Veneering" by Gordon Merrick. *Fine Woodworking,* October 1990; pp. 68-70.

"Visiting a Veneer Mill" by John Kriegshauser. *Fine Woodworking,* August 1991; pp. 42-45.

INDEX

A

Abrasive board:
  defined, 12
  making, 12
Acetone, cautions with, 140
Adam, Robert, mentioned, 4
Advanced Vacuum Bagging
    Techniques, cited, 130
Air pockets, formation of, 73
Aniline dyes:
  cautions with, 75
  for coloring veneer, 74-75
  mixing, 75
Apron, of demilune table. *See*
    Lamination, bent. Veneering.

B

Backerboard:
  defined, 41
  use of, 41
Bags, for vacuum press:
  attaching nipple to, 58
  backup for, 137
  cleaning, 142
  closure systems for, 58, 59, 66
  large holes in, repairing, 139, 140
  making, 57, 58
  patches for, 140
  pinholes in,
    finding, 136, 138
    repairing, 138
  repairing, during pressing, 137
  seams of,
    reinforcing, 142
    repairing, 141
  storing, 142
  troubleshooting, 136
  See also Presses, vacuum.
Bandsaws:
  single-point fence for, 40
  for slicing veneer, 40, 41
Bending forms:
  and air holes, 111
  bracing of, 122
  as caul, 121
  and inflatable bladders, 123
  making, 111, 113
  materials for, 108
  ribs of, 110, 111
  shallow, detail of, 122

single-part,
  assembly of, 96, 97
  blocks for, 97
  laminating on, 99
  layout of, 96
  materials for, 97
  template for, 96
skin for, 109
  attachment of, 113
  measuring for, 113
tall, platen for, 116, 117
testing of, 112
for top of coffee table, 122
two-part, 95
use of, for laminating, 114, 118
for veneering, 120
Bending plywood:
  as caul, 120
  characteristics of, 109, 110
  grain orientation of, 109
  and laminating, 114
  porosity of, 114
  for skin of bending form, 109, 110
Biscuit joiner, for slotting panels, 78
Biscuit joinery:
  with router, 80
  technique of, 78
Bladders, inflatable:
  in bending-form construction, 123
  detail of, 123
  discussed, 123
  finding, 123
  mentioned, 122
  in place of braces, 123
Blade drift:
  compensating for, 40
  defined, 40
Book box:
  construction of, 21
  making, to demonstrate hammer
    veneering, 20
Book-match:
  defined, 9
  discussed, 10
  example of, 10
  layout of, 22-24
Box:
  building, to demonstrate
    veneering, 42-51
  veneering edges of, 48, 49

Braces:
  and bending forms, 112
  inflatable bladders for, 122, 123
  need for, 112
  sizing, 112
  spacing, 112
Brayer. *See* Veneering, with roller.
Bubbles, repairing, 77

C

Cabinet scraper:
  discussed, 32
  for finishing, 32
  holder for, 32
  removing tape with, 82
  sharpening, 33
Camard, Florence (*Ruhlmann:*
    Master of Art Deco), cited, 6
Card table:
  assembly of, 82
  construction details of, 71
  edging, 78
  veneering of, with vacuum press,
    71
Cauls:
  and bending forms, 120
  melamine for, 74
  sizing, 75, 120
  thin, dangers of, 74
  for veneering curved legs, 102
cfm:
  defined, 62
  and pump ratings, 62
  See also Pumps, vacuum.
Chippendale, Thomas, mentioned, 4
Clamping, with vacuum press:
  advantages of, 128
  and glue-up, 128
  illustrated, 127
  platen for, 126
Closer strips, for vacuum bag, 58
Coffee table:
  assembly of, 124, 125
  construction details of, 107
  curved edges for, laminating of,
    124
  laminating base of, 114, 117
  making top for, 121, 122
  veneering, 118, 120
  veneering, with vacuum press,
    106

Cold creep:
    defined, 98
    results of, 98
Contact cement:
    for edgebanding, 86, 88
    See also Edgebanding.
CPVC pipe:
    as closer strips, 58
    for reinforcing seams, 142
    See also Bags, for vacuum press.
Crossbearers:
    defined, 39
    profiling, 39
Cross-gluing, defined, 72

D

Demilune table:
    assembly of, 105
    building of, to demonstrate
        vacuum veneering, 84-105
    construction details of, 85
    veneering of, 84
    See also Sunburst pattern.

E

Edgebanding:
    with contact cement, 86-88
    cutting, 86
    with hide glue, 86, 88-90
    veneer hammer for, 87, 89
Edges, curved:
    for coffee table, 124
    laminating of, 124
Edging:
    biscuit joinery with, 78
    for contrast, 78
    of tabletop, 78
Epoxy, for filling gaps, 34

F

Fences, single-point, for slicing
        veneer, 40
Filling:
    coloring of, 34
    epoxy for, 34
    of gaps, 34, 35
    marqueter's method of, 34
    paste fillers for, 34
    of pores, 35
    techniques of, 34
Finishing. *See* Veneer.
Flitch:
    defined, 7
    discussed, 10
French curves, and rib layout, 110

G

Gaps. *See* Filling.
Glues:
    application of, in vacuum press, 64
    hide,
        characteristics of, 16, 17
        for edgebanding, 86, 88-90
        preparing, 17, 18
        reactivating, with iron, 90
        storing, 18
        testing, 18, 19
        veneering with, 17
        working with, 16, 17
    for plugging leaks, 138
    polymerization of, defined, 56
    polyvinyl acetate adhesives
        (PVAs),
        for mechanical veneering, 42
        test piece for, 45, 46
    urea formaldehyde,
        experimenting with, 98
        for laminating, 98
        set time of, 98
    white, vacuum veneering with, 72
    See also Contact cement.
        Edgebanding. Veneering.
Golden rectangle:
    defined, 42
    discussed, 42
Gram strength:
    defined, 17
    See also Glues, hide.

H

Hammers, veneer:
    buying, 16
    making, 14-16
Hepplewhite, George, mentioned, 4
Hoadley, R. Bruce (*Understanding
        Wood*), cited, 6

I

Inlaying:
    with mechanical press, 49-51
    preparing for, 28, 30
    with roller, 30, 31
    with vacuum press:
        advantages of, 128
        glues with, 129
        mortise for, 129
        technique of, 128

J

Joining:
    caution with, 25
    methods of, 23, 25
    preparing for, 24, 119
    tools for, 11, 12, 25
    See also Sunburst pattern. Veneer.

K

Knife checks:
    defined, 7
    discussed, 8
    See also Veneer, loose side.

L

Laminating:
    of curved edges, 124
    of curved panels,
        materials for, 130
        without a form, 130, 131
    of multiple curves,
        and backer-grade veneer, 114
        and bending plywood, 114
        glues for, 114
        layout of, 114
        materials for, 114
        and platen size, 114
        in vacuum press, 117
        working time for, 117, 118
    in vacuum press,
        of bent lamination, 95, 98, 99
        of curved edges, 124
        of multiple curves, 114, 117
        without a form, 130, 131
    See also Bending forms.
        Laminations, bent.
Laminations, bent:
    forms for,
        single-part, 95
        two-part, 95
    glues for, 98
    glue-up of, 98
    pressing, in vacuum, 98, 99
    wood for, 95
    See also Bending forms.
Layout, method of, 23
Leaks, repairing, during pressing, 137
Legs:
    curved,
        cauls for, 102
        cutting veneer for, 103
        templates for, 102
        veneering, 102-105
    flat, veneering, 104
    tapered,
        template for, 80
        trimming veneer on, 82
        veneering, 80-82

M

Marking gauge:
    making, 96
    mentioned, 90
    and slicing veneer, 40
Marquetry (Ramond), cited, 6

Marquetry, defined, 49
Masking tape, to register veneer, 73
Masonite:
    and cutting veneer, 118
    as template, 80, 90, 91, 96, 102,
        103, 110,
    See also Bending forms. Legs,
        curved. Sunburst pattern.
Medium-density fiberboard (MDF):
    discussed, 18
    plugging, for screws, 49
    as substrate, 18, 20, 28, 72
    and table-leg hardware, 82
Melamine, as caul, 42, 74
Moisture content, and veneer, 13
Molding, veneering of. See Substrates.

O

Overhang, trimming. See Veneer,
    trimming.

P

Paint roller, for spreading glue, 73
Paint thinner:
    cautions with, 51
    and veneering, 51
Parquetry:
    defined, 49
    discussed, 49-51
    See also Inlaying.
Particleboard:
    and bending forms, 122
    as caul, 42
Paste fillers, and veneer, 35
Platens:
    for commercial presses, 63
    defined, 63
    for homemade vacuum presses, 63
    kerfing, 63
    making, 63
    material for, 63
    reducing size of, 101, 114
    and tall forms, 101
Plywood:
    as caul, 42
    for single-part bending form, 97
    as substrate, 72
    veneer orientation with, 72
    See also Bending plywood.
Pores. See Filling.

Presses:
    handscrew,
        discussed, 38
        use of, 45
        variation of, 38, 39
    hydraulic,
        advantages of, 38
        discussed, 38
        use of, 44
    mechanical,
        devices for, 36, 37, 39
        inlaying with, 51
    tools for, 12
    vacuum,
        accessories for, 67
        bags for, 67
        building, 56-62
        as clamping system, 126-128
        closure system for, 66, 67
        commercial, 62, 66, 67
        discussed, 62, 66
        elements of, 56
        example of, 55
        features of, 95
        as holding device, 133
        homemade, example of, 60
        how it works, 56
        and inflatable bladders, 123
        loading workpiece into, 75
        manufacturers of, 66
        and polymerization, 56
        purchasing, 66
        repairing bubbles in, 77
        silencer for, 61
        sources for, 67
        table for, 65, 68, 69
        testing, 64
        troubleshooting, 134, 135
    See also Inlaying. Laminating.
        Bags, for vacuum press. Pumps,
        for vacuum press.
Projects, for veneering. See Book box.
    Box. Card table. Coffee table.
    Demilune table.
Pumps, for vacuum press:
    commercial, 62, 66
    finding, 59
    maintenance of, 143
    rating, 62
    setting up, 59
    See also Presses, vacuum.

R

Ramond, Pierre (Marquetry), cited, 6
Red oak:
    as veneer substrate, 80
    for laminating, 95
Resawing. See Veneer, slicing.

Routers:
    trimming veneer with, 27
    See also Veneer, trimming.
Ruhlmann, Jacques-Emile,
    mentioned, 4
Ruhlmann: Master of Art Deco
    (Camard), cited, 6

S

Sand bags, hot, for veneering curved
    substrates, 53
Sheraton, Thomas, mentioned, 4
Slicing. See Veneer, slicing.
Slip-match:
    defined, 9
    discussed, 10
    example of, 10
Solid wood:
    and grain orientation with veneer,
        28, 29
    as substrate, 28
Stethoscope, homemade, for finding
    pinholes, 138
Substrates:
    concave, veneering of, 131, 132
    convex, veneering of, 132, 133
See also Medium-density fiberboard.
    Plywood. Solid wood.
Sunburst pattern:
    assembly of, 93
    cutting wedges for, 92
    design of, 91
    and grain symmetry, 92
    joining, 92, 93
    layout of, 86, 90, 91
    maintaining order of, 91
    substrate for, 86
    template for, 90, 91
    veneering of, in vacuum press, 94
Syringes:
    injecting glue with, 77
    See also Bubbles.

T

Table, for vacuum press:
    example of, 65, 68, 69
    making, 68, 69
    materials for, 68
    See also Presses, vacuum.
Templates. See Masonite. Bending
    forms.
Trimming. See Veneer.
Trowel, for spreading glue, 73

U

Understanding Wood (Hoadley),
cited, 6

V

Vacuum cleaner, use of, in vacuum
veneering, 62
Veneer:
backer grade,
coloring, 74
cutting method for, simple, 118
and laminating, 114
ordering, 114
in two-ply veneer, 76
use of, 74, 118
book-matching, 9
bubbles in, repairing, 77
burled, stabilizing of, 76
cutting,
multiple sheets, 103, 104
simple method, 118
for tapered legs, 81
tools for, 11, 12
traditional method, 23, 24
unorthodox method, 119
finishing,
discussed, 32
preparing for, 32
tools for, 32
joining, 11, 12, 23-25, 119
knife checks in, 7
laminating with, 114
laying out, for tapered legs, 81
layout of, 23
loose side, finding, 7, 8
moisture content of, 13
producing, illustration of, 5
rippled, 76
rotary cut, 6, 7
sawn, 6
sliced, 6, 7
slicing, on bandsaw, 40, 41
slip-matching, 9
smooth side, finding, 7, 8
on solid wood, and grain
orientation, 29
stabilizing, 13, 76, 119
storing, 13
substrates for, 28
trimming, 27, 28, 46, 47, 77, 82
two-ply, 76, 119
See also Aniline dyes. Book-match.
Joining. Slip-match.

Veneering:
accessories for, 67
of concave substrates, 131
of convex substrates, 132, 133
of curved legs, 102
of curves, 52, 53
with hammer,
of book box, 26
discussed, 14
and hide glue, 17, 18
and MDF, as substrate, 26
mentioned, 12
technique of, 18, 19, 26, 27
tools for, 12, 14, 17, 18
of legs. *See* Legs, curved. Legs,
tapered.
with mechanical presses,
cauls for, 42
of curves, 52-53
discussed, 36
glues for, 42
mentioned, 12
project for, 42
substrates for, 42
technique of, 42, 44, 45
of multiple curves, 118, 120, 121
with roller, 31
of solid wood, 28, 29
in vacuum press,
accessories for, 67
advantages of, 54
basic technique of, 70-75, 77,
80-82
of concave surfaces, 101
of convex surfaces, 100
of curved legs, 102-105
of demilune tabletop, *See*
Sunburst pattern.
discussed, 54
glues for, 64, 65
glues for, testing of, 64, 65
mentioned, 12
of multiple curves, 121
of multiple panels, 73, 74
of multiple sides, 73
projects for, 71 ,84, 106
of tapered legs, 80-82
tools for, 12
and vacuum cleaners, 62
See also Book box. Box. Card
table. Coffee table. Demilune
table. Inlaying. Marquetry.
Parquetry.
Venturi pump:
discussed, 61
for vacuum press, 61

W

Wacky wood. *See* Bending plywood.
Wax paper, and edgebanding, 87
Wiggle board. *See* Bending plywood.
Wood putty, filling with, 113
Woodworkers Alliance for Rainforest
Protection (WARP), mentioned,
72

Editor: THOMAS C. McKENNA

Designer: HENRY ROTH

Layout artist: SUZANNA M. YANNES

Photographer, except where noted: DAVID SHATH SQUARE

Illustrator: VINCENT BABAK

Typeface: GARAMOND

Paper: WARREN PATINA MATTE, 70 LB., NEUTRAL pH

Printer: QUEBECOR PRINTING/HAWKINS, NEW CANTON, TENNESSEE